BAD
HOA

Bad HOA

The Homeowner's Guide
to Going to War and
Reclaiming Your Power

Luke S. Carlson, Esq.

WREN HOUSE
press

BAD HOA
The Homeowner's Guide to Going to War and Reclaiming Your Power
First Edition

ISBN   979-8-9912039-8-2   *Hardcover*
       979-8-9912039-7-5   *Paperback*
       979-8-9912039-6-8   *Ebook*

This book is dedicated to my family.

*Thank you for reminding me daily
that home isn't where you live,
but who you're with.*

LEGAL DISCLAIMER

This publication, *Bad HOA: The Homeowner's Guide to Going to War and Reclaiming Your Power*, exclusively serves as a general informational resource directed to the public at large, for general knowledge. This book does not offer personal advice regarding the legal problems of any specific person. This book is not intended as personalized legal counsel and there is no attorney-client relationship between author and reader. Should you require actual legal support, you are advised to solicit the services of a qualified legal professional. The author and/or publisher do not function as your attorney.

We have meticulously surveyed the landscape of homeowners association (HOA) law to present a comprehensive general informational overview in this book. However, laws are subject to jurisdictional variations. We disclaim any responsibility for potential inaccuracies or misinterpretations resulting from the general information provided herein. This book is a general informational resource and does not attempt to conform to specific laws and regulations governing homeowners associations in individual states.

The names and situations presented in this book are fictional representations created to explore and address general themes and scenarios within the context of homeowners associations. Any resemblance to real-life events, individuals, or entities is purely coincidental.

Consult an attorney or other qualified professional for legal advice about your circumstances. The author and publisher issue a disclaimer, explicitly absolving themselves of any accountability for repercussions, losses, or damages arising from the content in this book. By reading this book, you agree not to attribute any adverse consequences to the author or publisher.

P.S. A lawyer wrote this book, so of course there is a disclaimer!

Contents

"It does not take a majority to prevail...but rather an irate, tireless minority, keen on setting brushfires of freedom in the minds of men."

—SAMUEL ADAMS

Introduction

When my mother-in-law wanted to get married, I knew just the place for a picture-perfect ceremony.

Down the road from my house in Southern California lies a lush greenbelt overlooking the ocean. It's a popular spot in the community, often hosting concerts and other celebrations and offering a ready-made vista for any couple ready to tie the knot. Wanting to give her mother an unforgettable wedding, my wife submitted a request to our homeowners association to use the space and waited for approval.

"We don't reserve the park," an HOA representative informed my wife via email. Their terse response was direct but ambiguous.

Ever the optimist, my wife interpreted the statement to mean that the greenbelt was first come, first served. As long as no one else was using the space at that time, she reasoned, we could use it for the wedding. So, that's exactly what we did.

About a month after the wedding, we received a letter from the HOA requesting our presence at a hearing. The HOA board members demanded an explanation as to why we had hosted a wedding at the park without their permission. Apparently, they did not allow access to the greenbelt for private events—although this "rule" was not in any of the governing documents.

Interesting.

These board members didn't know it then, but this wasn't my first rodeo. Quickly, I had one of my law firm's attorneys draft a response. We politely identified the ambiguity in the HOA's reply to the initial request and lack of any language in the governing documents prohibiting such activities. As we explained, we had taken the response to mean we had open access to the greenbelt and requested that the board withdraw the complaint.

A few days later, the matter was dropped. No harm, no foul.

In an ideal world, this is how all misunderstandings with HOAs should go. I'm not some Rambo attorney eager to steamroll HOAs just because I can. I'm fully prepared to own up to my mistakes when I know what they are, and I expect my HOA to do the same. That's why, as politely as possible, we extended an olive branch—written on my firm's letterhead—explaining the miscommunication. Seeing that we were both civil and serious, the HOA complied, and we all emerged from the interaction unscathed.

Unfortunately, in another community, in another homeowners association, for another homeowner, this exact situation could have escalated into something far worse. Since you are reading this book, I'm betting that you are experiencing more negative outcomes in your community.

TROUBLE IN THE NEIGHBORHOOD

Targeted harassment. Ambiguous fees and citations. Willful neglect of public spaces. These are the telltale signs of a bad HOA—and they're all too familiar in communities nationwide.

Issues like these undermine the peace and harmony you were promised when you first moved into your community. The neighborhood HOA you thought would protect and serve you has instead turned into an antagonistic fiefdom that threatens not only one of your most valuable possessions—your home—but also your quality of life (not to mention your sanity). The HOA might preach harmony, shared responsibilities, and an idyllic vision, but under the rug lies a dirty secret: no one's steering the ship properly.

In my experience as an attorney exclusively representing homeowners in HOA disputes, I've learned that homeowners associations are only as good as the people who sit on their boards and the professionals advising them. Some board members are power-hungry Tyrants (an archetype we'll meet in Chapter 3), weaponizing their positions and hiding behind codes and bylaws to shore up their despotic rule. Others are Fools who are simply ignorant, incompetent, or negligent. And while the incompetent often don't mean any harm, they also don't know what they are doing or understand how their actions create an absolute nightmare for others.

Whatever the case, and whatever their intent, the result is the same: a confused, frustrated community of homeowners unsure how to protect their rights—or even what their rights are.

I get it. There's a lot of fine print to navigate. Between your purchase agreements, the HOA's governing documents, the HOA's fiduciary obligations, and any laws enacted by your state, it's easy to feel like you're swimming in a sea of legalese. How can you fight back against your bad HOA when you can't articulate or even pinpoint exactly what it might have done wrong?

We'll answer that question in the chapters that follow. But first, let's get one thing clear.

An HOA is designed to benefit homeowners and the community. Period. If your HOA's actions (or inactions) cause you or your community harm, you are within your rights to fight back. Fortunately, you don't have to go it alone.

ADVOCATING FOR THE VOICELESS

I never expected to represent homeowners in their struggle against bad HOAs.

In the mid- to late nineties, I was an avid surfer in Florida. Somewhat competitive, I traveled quite a bit. Sometime in early adulthood, in my pursuit of chasing waves, I ended up in California, where I also returned to school. My interest in political theory gave way to an interest in law. I was fascinated by the art of persuasion and argument, and I loved bringing these skills to bear on complex social and legal problems. Plus, the legal field was highly competitive—not unlike the environment I had thrived in during my surfing days.

After passing the bar in 2009, I cut my teeth practicing real estate and business law. While my firm, LS Carlson Law, focused primarily on complex business and real estate litigation, we kept getting HOA work from homeowners because few attorneys would touch their cases. At first, we didn't understand the extent of the demand for good representation in that sector. We figured we'd get a case here, a case there, and nothing more. Soon, though, we came to realize just how deep the rabbit hole went.

As an impartial civil attorney adept at marshaling hard evidence, I have concluded that homeowners generally have a bad opinion of HOAs. Research backs this up. According to a 2024 Rocket Mortgage survey, 57 percent of homeowners living under an HOA aren't happy with their experience.[1] I can personally vouch for that number. If anything, it seems a little low.

Whenever I tell someone I represent homeowners in HOA disputes, their eyes light up with anger. "Have I got a story for you!" they say. Typically, these stories involve rogue board members, property damage, unscrupulous fines, demands for endless hearings, or combative board meetings. I've even heard stories of an HOA attempting to sell a homeowner's home right out from under them, due to fines that were levied against the homeowner illegally.

Often these stories are accompanied by an overwhelming feeling of helplessness. "I've gone to the board seven times, and they basically told me to go screw myself," one memorable client told us during our initial meeting. "I don't know what to do. I've called around to a bunch of lawyers, and no one knows how to fight back."

After hearing story after story like this, we rolled up our sleeves and went all in on representing homeowners against bad HOAs. At first, most HOAs we encountered were arrogant and reckless. They were used to steamrolling the little people in their nice, neat kingdoms and had never encountered a team of lawyers who actually

---

1   Jessica Edmondson, "57% of HOA Residents Don't Like Having an HOA," Rocket Mortgage, March 4, 2024, https://www.rocketmortgage.com/learn/assessing-the-association.

knew how to advocate for homeowners. We caught them flat-footed. We entered the fight with comprehensive knowledge of the relevant state laws and regulations. We understood how to interpret HOAs' governing documents. We knew how to strategically and aggressively leverage the legal system to our clients' advantage. HOAs through-out California realized we weren't bluffing and began to play ball after we handed many of them some truly embar-rassing losses.

Soon, word of our victories spread like wildfire, both among homeowners and in the legal community. As our reputation grew, so did our firm. Today, LS Carlson Law has offices in both California and Florida, where we have helped several thousand households resolve their dis-putes with their bad HOAs. And that's just the beginning. With this book, I hope to empower thousands more.

To be clear: this is not a book on how to run an effec-tive HOA. There are plenty of books written by board members for board members, and the world doesn't need another one.

Instead, this is a resource for homeowners who, for far too long, have needed somewhere to turn when their relationship with their HOA goes bad. Even for the most dedicated self-advocate, few resources exist to teach homeowners how to navigate a contentious battle with their HOA. There are no step-by-step guides, no advice on how to hire a lawyer, and no proven tips on how to kick a problematic HOA board in the mouth...figuratively speaking, of course.

That's why I wrote this book.

Bad HOA is a resource to empower homeowners who have been caught in the crossfire of an unjust, confusing war with their HOA when they don't know how to fight back. If you've ever gone cross-eyed reading your HOA's covenants, conditions, and restrictions (CC&Rs), this book is for you. If you've ever searched the web into the wee hours of the morning to learn how to take on your HOA without going bankrupt, this book is for you. If you've ever wished that a particularly nosy board member would just leave you alone, this book is for you.

If you're reading this, you're undoubtedly at a crossroads. Down one road, you can choose to tolerate your HOA's unchecked abuse. Down the other road, you can stand up and fight.

I know which path I'd choose.

Sometimes, war is necessary to win peace. Your HOA nightmare will only go away if you demand and fight for justice.

Consider this book your battle plan for understanding, asserting, and safeguarding your rights against bad HOAs. In the following chapters, we'll explore a variety of topics: how HOAs operate, the reasons they often go sour, and the methodology and legal process to challenge them.

There's a lot to cover, but the payoff is worth it. As you'll see, while your HOA might try a bunch of smoke and mirrors to silence you, the solutions for beating it can be relatively simple. Anyone can take on a bad HOA. It's just a matter of knowing which levers to pull.

Before we dive in, here is a warning: my law firm, LS Carlson Law, PC, practices HOA law in California and Florida. Each state has its own set of specific rules and regulations designed to protect homeowners and homeowners associations. I have written this book as a general guide for taking on bad HOAs regardless of your state or zip code, but every jurisdiction is different, and some of this advice may not apply. As you work to empower yourself, I encourage you to understand the lay of the land before taking any direct action and to consult a legal expert in your jurisdiction whenever possible.

With that out of the way, let's get started with some fundamentals.

"To be prepared for war is one of the most effective means of preserving peace."

— GEORGE WASHINGTON

The ABCs of HOAs

B ETWEEN 1970 AND 2020, THE NUMBER OF HOUS-
ing units governed by a homeowners association in
the United States grew from 700,000 to 27 million,
an 839 percent increase.[2] By 2024, about 75.5 million
Americans lived in a community governed by an HOA—
representing more than 30 percent of the US housing
stock.[3]

---

2   David Bitton, "HOA Statistics for 2024—Making Sense of Benchmarks,"
    DoorLoop, June 23, 2024, https://www.doorloop.com/blog/hoa-statistics.
3   Melissa Dittmann Tracey, "Study: Homeowners Associations Are Booming,"
    REALTOR® Magazine, March 14, 2024, https://www.nar.realtor/magazine/
    real-estate-news/study-homeowners-associations-are-booming.

Perhaps unsurprisingly, many HOA-governed communities are in the nation's biggest, fastest-growing states: California, Texas, and Florida. Homeowner experiences with HOAs vary by location. Each state has laws and regulations regarding the formation and conduct of HOAs, and each state has a different percentage of HOAs relative to its overall number of homes. If you're buying in a high-percentage state like California, you might feel like you can't throw a rock without hitting a community governed by an HOA. (And, for the record, I advise against throwing rocks near any neighborhood as a general rule.)

This isn't to say that homes outside the governance of an HOA aren't available. However, available homes outside the jurisdiction of an HOA are generally less desirable, especially in the bigger states like California, Texas, and Florida. They're in older neighborhoods, within city limits, usually smaller and with fewer modern conveniences, and built for a different decade with different aesthetics, professional needs, and family dynamics.

Here's what all this means for you as a homeowner. Suppose you want to live in a modern home with modern amenities in any of the nation's fastest-growing population centers. In that case, it's increasingly likely that you will buy a home in an HOA. If you're reading this book, chances are you already live in an HOA...and are less than happy with the experience.

But what is an HOA, how does it work, and how does living in one affect you as a homeowner? With so many HOAs now governing communities, it's alarming that so few people know what they are or what they do.

In this chapter, we'll cover HOA Fundamentals 101: what an HOA is, how it works, and its intended benefits and unintended challenges. Through learning the process by which HOAs are formed and the purpose they are intended to serve, homeowners like you can better understand your rights and responsibilities within your community.

First, a note on how to read this chapter. The goal here is to provide you with a working knowledge of all the basics of an HOA. Presented together, it's a lot of information to wade through. Don't worry—you don't need to memorize everything, and there is no test at the end. Give this material a good read-through now, and then bookmark it for later when you need a little refresher.

WHAT IS A HOMEOWNERS ASSOCIATION?

A homeowners association is a legal entity established to manage and govern a community of homes or condominiums. A planned community or subdivision developer typically establishes an HOA, which is then responsible for managing the community's finances, maintaining common areas, and enforcing the CC&Rs.

WHAT IS THE PURPOSE OF A HOMEOWNERS ASSOCIATION?

In essence, the purpose of a homeowners association is to create and maintain a well-managed, harmonious, and desirable living environment for all residents. By establishing rules, resolving disputes, maintaining common areas, managing finances, and fostering a sense of community, HOAs play a vital role in shaping the quality of life within residential neighborhoods and condominium complexes.

HOAs are supposed to *help* their community members and bring greater peace and prosperity to everyone. With comprehensive CC&Rs, a capable board, and a competent management company, an HOA can meet these goals incredibly well. Here's how HOAs are intended to fulfill this purpose.

COMMUNITY GOVERNANCE

HOAs are governing bodies that establish and enforce the rules and regulations that govern the community's use and the appearance of properties. For instance, an HOA might require you to mow and edge your front lawn or limit the number of guests you invite to the community pool. These rules, outlined in the governing documents, are intended to promote a happy, harmonious community and protect the homeowners' interests and real estate values. No one wants to live near the neighbor with the parted-out car in the front yard. Written and enforced correctly, CC&Rs prevent one homeowner from devaluing another's property.

PROPERTY MAINTENANCE AND ENHANCEMENT

One of the major functions of an HOA is to oversee the maintenance and upkeep of common areas and amenities within the community. This includes landscaping, road maintenance, snow removal, and repairs to amenities and shared facilities like swimming pools, clubhouses, dog parks, and playgrounds. By ensuring that common areas are well maintained and aesthetically pleasing—for instance, that they are safe, functional, and good-looking—HOAs help enhance property values and create a desirable living environment for residents.

ENFORCEMENT OF COMMUNITY STANDARDS

HOAs are like the neighborhood watchdogs for architectural rules and community standards. They ensure all residents' homes look nice and fit the neighborhood's unique style. These standards may include requirements or restrictions on exterior modifications and colors, signage, landscaping, and usage of specific materials. By maintaining consistent standards and enforcing compliance among homeowners, HOAs help protect property values and promote a cohesive aesthetic within the community. You may love your neighbor's enthusiastic Christmas spirit during the winter holiday season. However, if you see those same faded and ragged decorations still up by Easter, you might feel a little different.

FINANCIAL MANAGEMENT

HOAs are responsible for managing the community's financial affairs, including collecting assessments and dues from homeowners, budgeting for operating expenses and reserve funds, and hiring contractors and vendors for maintenance and repair work. By prudently managing financial resources, HOAs ensure that the community's infrastructure and amenities remain in good condition and that funds are available for future capital improvements and unforeseen expenses, like fixing a broken front gate after a tree falls on it during a storm.

DISPUTE RESOLUTION AND COMMUNITY ENGAGEMENT

HOAs provide a structured framework for resolving disputes among homeowners and addressing concerns related to rule violations, property maintenance issues, and neighborly conflicts, such as who pays to fix a shared privacy fence. Through a variety of dispute-resolution options, HOAs seek to foster a sense of fairness and accountability within the community. Additionally, HOAs often organize social events, community activities, and volunteer initiatives to promote neighborly interaction and community spirit, like concerts or potluck dinners.

HOW ARE HOMEOWNERS ASSOCIATIONS FORMED?

A good way for a city to defer costs is to delegate the infrastructure and upkeep of a large chunk of land to an HOA. The typical story goes something like this. The city has a big undeveloped plot of land. A developer comes in and says, "I want to develop this land with residential homes."

"Okay, great," the city says, "but we don't want to pay for the construction and maintenance of public spaces in that neighborhood. We may not even want to handle utilities like trash collection."

"Fine," says the developer. They then agree to include a homeowners association to govern the neighborhood. The developer establishes the neighborhood's HOA through the HOA's governing documents, helping to maintain the specific aesthetic vision that's being sold to a particular demographic of buyers—for instance, single-family units with a modern design. Essentially, the HOA's job is to set and maintain the community's branding.

Then, if someone buys into the community, they must agree to uphold the community's aesthetic standards, maintain a neat and clean appearance, and refrain from doing anything that would destroy or devalue their neighbors' property. For instance, if you have a beautiful, well-maintained home, but your neighbor has a rusted car in their front yard sitting on a throne of concrete blocks and weeds, your lovely home is immediately devalued. By preventing such dynamics, the developer helps to keep property values stable until they've built and sold all the homes.

Typically, the homeowners take over the HOA's operations after the developer has sold all (or a majority) of the homes and moved on. Using their dues as capital, the community works together to pay for the upkeep of the common areas, control their aesthetic vision for the community, and maintain their property values.

That's it in a nutshell. The following subsections will further break down the critical steps in forming and documenting an HOA. These steps happen in the order listed and can take one to five years to complete. Legal requirements are an ongoing issue, as state laws may change from year to year, necessitating an update to the HOA's governing documents and processes.

DEVELOPER CONTROL

In most cases, the residential community developer establishes the HOA to manage and govern the community's common areas and amenities and establish rules and regulations for homeowners.

CREATION OF GOVERNING DOCUMENTS

As part of the development process, the developer drafts and records a set of documents that govern the HOA's operations. Typically, these include the following:

1. **Articles of Incorporation**. This document establishes the HOA as a legal entity and outlines its purpose, powers, and structure. It is filed with the state government and typically includes basic information such as the HOA's name, address, purpose, and duration of existence. This makes an HOA a separate entity from the city and allows it to police itself.

2. **Covenants, Conditions, and Restrictions (CC&Rs)**. The CC&Rs outline the rights and obligations of homeowners within the community, as well as any restrictions on land use, architectural standards, maintenance responsibilities, and limitations on activities such as renting or leasing. They are binding on all homeowners within the community and enforceable legally.

3. **Bylaws**. A community's bylaws establish the rules and procedures governing the operation of the HOA. This document typically covers topics such as the board of directors' composition and powers, meetings and election procedures, homeowners' voting rights, and financial management practices. The bylaws provide the framework for how the HOA conducts its business and interacts with its members.

4. **Rules and Regulations**. These documents supplement the CC&Rs and bylaws by providing specific guidelines and requirements for homeowners to follow. These rules may address issues such as parking, noise, pet ownership, landscaping, and use of shared facilities. While the CC&Rs and bylaws establish the HOA's overarching framework, the rules and regulations provide additional detail and clarity on specific matters.

If you've already moved into an HOA-run community and haven't reviewed these documents, consider this a friendly reminder to acquaint yourself with them. It may not be the most compelling reading, but knowledge is power.

TRANSFER OF CONTROL

Once a certain number of homes within the community have been sold, the developer typically transfers control of the HOA to the homeowners. This transition usually occurs when a certain percentage of homes have been sold or a specified period has elapsed since the community was established.

HOMEOWNER CONTROL

When a homeowners association is handed over to the homeowners, the community's first order of business is to elect a board of directors. These folks are in charge of running the HOA and making good choices for the community. They enforce the rules and bylaws, handle the money, and address homeowners' problems or needs.

LEGAL REQUIREMENTS

It's important to note that the formation and operation of HOAs are subject to state laws and regulations, which may vary depending on the jurisdiction. In many states, HOAs must register with the appropriate governmental agency and comply with specific legal requirements regarding governance, financial reporting, and dispute resolution. These state laws and regulations are the same as those that govern nonprofit corporations, real estate, and common interest communities. Additionally, local ordinances and zoning regulations may also impact the operation of an HOA, particularly regarding issues such as land use, property maintenance, and noise control. HOAs must ensure that their actions and policies always comply with applicable laws and regulations.

WHAT ARE THE KEY COMPONENTS OF A HOMEOWNERS ASSOCIATION?

A few key components define an HOA and allow it to fulfill its goal of serving homeowners. Even if the particulars differ from community to community, all HOAs will have the following.

GOVERNING DOCUMENTS

HOAs operate under governing documents like articles of incorporation, CC&Rs, bylaws, and rules and regulations. These documents detail homeowners' rights and responsibilities, as well as the HOA board's powers.

MEMBERSHIP

When you purchase a home in a community governed by an HOA, you automatically become a member of the association. As a member, you are required to abide by the HOA's rules and regulations and pay regular assessments to cover the cost of common expenses.

BOARD OF DIRECTORS

A volunteer board of directors elected by the homeowners manages the typical HOA. As the community's governing head and primary decision-making body, the board enforces rules, oversees finances, and hires vendors for maintenance and repairs. This is where the buck stops.

ASSESSMENTS

Homeowners are typically required to pay regular assessments, also known as dues or fees, to the HOA. These assessments fund the association's operating expenses, such as maintenance of common areas, landscaping, security, insurance, and reserve funds for future repairs and capital improvements. These assessments function much like a state or federal tax that pays for the upkeep and construction of the HOA's public utilities and spaces. In effect, by buying a home, you become a citizen of a tiny republic.

COMMUNITY AMENITIES

Many HOAs provide amenities and services for residents, such as swimming pools, tennis courts, parks, clubhouse facilities, and landscaping. The HOA's board of directors maintains these amenities through the monthly assessments collected from each homeowner in the community. If the board is considering any major changes to these amenities, such as improvements or new construction, it is typically required to seek community feedback first.

WHAT ARE THE CHALLENGES OF LIVING IN AN HOA-RUN COMMUNITY?

While HOAs are intended to benefit residents, if you're reading this book, you know that's not always the case. Even relatively well-run HOAs can present challenges to homeowners. These challenges exist for any type of governing body, large or small. Still, residents feel the impacts much more quickly and personally when such a body operates at the scale of a single community.

After this chapter, we'll explore the friction points that HOAs pose in much greater detail. Typically, these challenges fall into one of the following categories.

RESTRICTIONS ON PROPERTY USE

HOAs may impose restrictions on homeowners regarding the use of their properties, such as limitations on exterior modifications, signage, and landscaping. To protect the community's functionality, the HOA must make aesthetic decisions with the majority in mind. However, these restrictions aren't always popular. For instance, in drought-conscious areas, HOAs often restrict landscaping and trees to native or drought-tolerant species, which might not fit a homeowner's desire to plant a beautiful but invasive Bradford pear tree.

ASSESSMENTS, FEES, AND FINES

Homeowners contribute regular assessments to the HOA. The amount and frequency vary based on the community's finances and needs. HOAs can also legally use citations and fines to enforce community regulations, punishing people who commit infractions or break rules. If I just triggered your PTSD by describing these challenges, you're not alone. The amount, timing, and fairness of these fees—and the communication surrounding them—represent major points of conflict for many homeowners.

GOVERNANCE AND DECISION-MAKING

Some homeowners may feel frustrated by the decision-making process within the HOA, particularly if they disagree with the board's actions, inactions, or policies—or if they believe they weren't properly notified or consulted on changes to policies or decisions. Proper community feedback on decisions affecting the whole community can make the difference between feeling like you live in a republic or a kingdom.

HOW CAN I AVOID BUYING A HOME WITH A BAD HOA?

Once you are in a position to review your new HOA's governing documents at closing, it's often too far into the home-buying process to feel like you can reasonably back out—though that could be an option if you don't think you can live with the regulations outlined.

If you spend a few hours researching your intended HOA *before* making an offer on your dream home, you'll be in a better position to accept its conditions when you sign on the dotted line. After all, if you see signs that you might be about to purchase in a community with an HOA plagued by lawsuits and maintenance issues, then your new home's equity—and your peace of mind—could suffer.

Before you buy, here are a few questions you can answer to determine whether you've found a community you want to live in.

ARE THE CC&Rs KEPT UP TO DATE?

The first writers of a community's governing documents are not the current residents of that community. The developers who built the community wrote those documents. As such, they put rules in place to build and sell the homes as quickly as possible.

Governing documents should, and often do, evolve with the times, the changing needs, and the values of the families who live in a community, but old rules sometimes get held over. For example, some of the first CC&Rs authored in the 1950s and 1960s stipulated that homeowners could not sell their homes to people of Jewish or African descent. Most communities have struck these rules from subsequent versions of their governing documents. However, antiquated and illegal provisions might still exist in communities that don't update their CC&Rs regularly.

Of course, problems with the CC&Rs are rarely this drastic. In many communities, the ineffective CC&Rs could be as simple as a requirement to keep and maintain a lush green lawn—even though persistent drought restrictions in the region make that requirement a practical impossibility. However, replacing this requirement with a mandate for xeriscaping would require a rewrite and board approval of that part of the CC&Rs.

ARE THERE RECENT COMPLAINTS AGAINST THE HOA?

You could also peruse your state court's website, doing a name search on your potential association to see how many lawsuits have been filed by or against it in the last few years. If there have been any lawsuits, you could pay a few dollars to pull the complaint to see how aggressive the HOA was in filing suits against its community or vice versa.

In addition to researching the HOA's legal history, there are good old online reviews. Interpreting reviews always requires a grain of salt, as some aren't credible. However, if you scan enough reviews, you should notice trends in your potential HOA's behavior.

HOW DOES THE NEIGHBORHOOD LOOK?

Drive the neighborhood and check out the common areas. Doing so can reveal much about how this HOA handles its day-to-day tasks. If fences are falling down, the playground equipment is broken, the landscaping is overgrown, and yard cars are popping up like weeds, then the HOA is clearly not doing its job.

Of course, you might also be repelled by the opposite. If you value your right to paint and landscape your home however you want but see that every home in the neighborhood has a white door and a lawn mowed to exactly one inch high, then that might also be a sign you don't want to deal with this HOA.

HOAS ARE A GOOD THING...UNTIL THEY'RE NOT

At the simplest level, HOAs are intended to be equalizers, ensuring that one bad apple can't spoil the whole barrel without consequences. The compromise of an HOA is

giving up the freedom to make certain kinds of maintenance and aesthetic choices, in exchange for the benefit of
the entire community and a higher payoff later. However,
while rules might be made with good intentions, as we'll
see throughout this book, those good intentions are not
always well executed.

I'm not against the intended goal of HOAs. It makes a lot
of sense to establish guardrails for a shared environment
that expects everyone, when literally buying in, to also fig-
uratively buy into agreed-upon standards of maintenance,
aesthetics, and neighborly behavior for the sake of everyone's bottom line. In that way, an HOA can absolutely act
for the greater good of the community.

Having an HOA also ensures the timely maintenance of
shared spaces and amenities. It could take years for a city's
public pool to secure the funds and go through the red tape
to get fixed, but an HOA has a ready reserve of homeowner
dues and minimal red tape. One maintenance request
later, a contractor could be taking care of that unseemly
and unsafe crack in the pool decking. And home buyers
now expect walkable amenities—like pools, playgrounds,
and dog parks—as well as prompt fixes to safety issues,
like dead trees and burned-out streetlights.

In all these ways, a well-appointed and well-maintained
community is a desirable community. People want to live
there, which also means people want to buy there. If you
want or need to sell your home, you won't have long to wait

for a buyer willing to pay top dollar, giving you a nice little profit on the investment you made five to ten years ago.

Of course, as you know, this ideal doesn't always reflect reality. Enforcing the rules falls to bureaucracy. And like any bureaucracy, your HOA could be run by fallible people who don't necessarily have the training or checks and balances required for good governance. Indeed, HOA boards can become chaotic or overly focused on rules instead of their main goal: improving the properties in the community and the lives of the homeowners.

It's a lofty goal, and when an HOA works and everyone feels they've been dealt with fairly, it's wonderful. But sometimes a homeowners association doesn't work in the way it's supposed to, and the utopia you thought you bought into becomes a dystopian nightmare. The home that was supposed to bring a sense of community and financial growth instead brings animosity and financial and legal hardship. If that's the case, it's safe to say that you have become the victim of a bad HOA.

KEY TAKEAWAYS

- HOAs are run by a democratically elected board that must enforce and uphold legal standards and restrictions designed to benefit all homeowners in the community.

- Living under an HOA's rules has benefits and challenges, but in a well-functioning HOA, the benefits outweigh the challenges.

- A dysfunctional HOA often displays telltale signs that prospective homeowners can observe before they decide to buy in a particular community.

"Bad men need nothing more to compass their ends, than that good men should look on and do nothing."

—JOHN STUART MILL

Why Do HOAs Go Bad?

ONCE UPON A TIME, A TYPICAL HOMEOWNER named Frank bought his dream home. This beauty checked all the boxes. Established, planned community? Check. Neighbors with festive holiday decorations? Check. Large trees, landscaped yards, and a greenbelt for hiking and walking dogs? Check, check, check.

Upon closing, Frank received a copy of his HOA's governing documents. He had no idea whether his HOA was good or bad, how it was run, or what it did. Still, he assumed the board members were at least competent. Why would he have any reason to suspect otherwise?

As he began to flip through the CC&Rs, though, he got a nagging feeling. The rules were written in 1989—although they read much older than that. Frank didn't realize just how big of a red flag this was at the time. His municipal, state, and federal laws had changed quite a bit since 1989, and the HOA hadn't been keeping up to date with the changes. If Frank had breathed deeply, he would have caught a whiff of the legal neglect coating the antiquated rules he was wrongfully expected to follow, a neglect that didn't bode well. As he would soon find out, an HOA that is negligent about updating its CC&Rs is often negligent about many other things, such as enforcing general maintenance and fulfilling fiduciary responsibilities.

In the months and years that followed, Frank constantly grappled with the board—whether to fight unfair citations, make requests rarely honored, or seek transparency regarding how the board managed the HOA's funds. Clearly, at some point in the past, the HOA in Frank's neighborhood had taken a turn for the worse.

But why? What causes a good HOA to go bad?

That's what we'll explore in this chapter. There are a few key reasons why boards go bad, and most of them have their root in how HOAs are set up, such as the volunteer nature of the board and the ethics and conduct of the management companies hired to carry out the HOA's duties. Most of the time, your worst suspicions are true: the problem is them, not you.

Fortunately, with a basic understanding of the underlying problems that lead to bad HOAs, you will have the foundation to understand how an HOA might respond when you push back—and how you can begin to leverage the system to your advantage.

REASON #1: VOLUNTEER BOARDS

The first thing to understand about why HOAs go bad is that their board positions are voluntary. Any member of the community is free to run for an open seat. It's a big, important position, but typically, few people are interested.

But why is that? A few reasons:

1. There may be only a couple hundred households in the community from which to draw qualified candidates.
2. Generally, any board member must be a property owner and resident of the community, which further limits the pool of qualified candidates.
3. The person has to pay enough attention to community politics to know when and how to run for the board and get elected.
4. The person must be interested in a volunteer position with the same responsibilities as a C-suite role.

As you can imagine, these limitations narrow the talent pool. When we put up a job posting to add to our team of exceptional lawyers, like most law firms, we receive a great deal of high-quality interest. When it comes time for my HOA board to find a new director, you'd think the whole community would chime in. Instead, we get Jeff and Tom, two guys who might just be there for the snacks. When only two people raise their (Cheeto-dusted) hands, it's not exactly a recipe for success!

If the voluntary nature of these positions narrows the talent pool so dramatically, why not make these paid positions? Put simply, because they're not allowed to be. Mandates differ by state, but generally, all HOA board positions are required to be filled by volunteers. This means official onboarding or training is left to the whims of your particular board. If the board has no established system for outgoing or existing board members to coach newcomers, the incoming directors may have no idea how to conduct themselves. It can be a sink-or-swim scenario, requiring new directors to train themselves through available resources or existing documentation.

The key here is that people volunteering for these positions must do all that research on their own unpaid time. This means that learning the job is typically low on their priority list—a few steps down from their career, hobbies, and family. For most people, reading dry management how-tos for a position that will never lead to financial or career advancement is not the definition of a good time.

Of course, in a perfect world, each board member would take their volunteer job and responsibilities seriously and demonstrate the initiative to do right by people. In practice, however, that's rare. On a board of five directors, often only one member is genuinely altruistic and wants to do a good job. The rest may have generally good intentions but are often apathetic when it comes to actually fulfilling their duties.

This built-in apathy has a compounding effect on the well-being of the community. An apathetic board is an ineffective board, and an ineffective board is less likely to ensure that its third-party management company is doing its part. Taken together, you have all the ingredients you need to create one hell of a dumpster fire.

New homeowners like Frank aren't aware that these dumpster fires are possible, let alone common. Often by the time they sniff out a problem, they've already signed the paperwork, moved into the neighborhood, and begun to build a new life there. Once they realize there's an issue, they're typically unsure what to do about it. After all, how do you put out a dumpster fire when you don't understand its root causes? Keep reading.

REASON #2: THE SPECTRUM OF INACTION

As discussed in the last chapter, the board of directors makes all the decisions for an HOA. Often, the board will then outsource the actual running of the HOA to a third-party management company.

Like any leadership team, the quality of an HOA's board of directors sits along a spectrum. There are good boards, bad boards, so-so boards, and everything in between. Bad boards typically skew toward the extreme ends of the spectrum. They either don't act or overreact. We'll cover the harms of overreaction in the next chapter. But for now, let's tackle the problem of inaction.

When board members don't act, it is often due to sheer laziness, incompetence, or both. Why? Typically, no one has ever challenged them. They've gone unchecked.

Suppose the problem doesn't affect any board members personally, and there are no repercussions for ignoring their tasks. In that case, they tend to let it persist—*until* the homeowner or coalition of homeowners brings the issue to their door and holds their feet to the contractual fire. For instance, the community pool is broken. The board members were elected and empowered to enforce the CC&Rs, including maintaining the pool. It's time they do their job, or else.

Sometimes, though, the board's reason for inaction isn't laziness but ignorance. The board members aren't bad actors. They don't know what they are responsible for or how to fulfill those responsibilities. In these cases, politely reminding them of what they must do and why can sometimes get the job done. Again, this scenario requires you to act and enforce your rights as homeowner.

Other times, it's not the board that's lazy or ignorant, but the management company. If the management company is dropping the ball and not keeping the board informed, even an otherwise knowledgeable and competent board can be caught flat-footed. They have no idea there's a problem, because the company they hired to take care of any problems has never mentioned anything (which is often the case). Suppose the board decides to outsource its responsibilities to a management company that is downright negligent, prioritizing profit over proper service. In that case, this company might filter out complaints that the board absolutely needs to address.

A negligent management company doesn't excuse the board from culpability. It's the board's job to understand how the management company is performing. If board members do not provide proper oversight and monitoring to ensure accountability of the management company acting on their behalf, the fault still lies with them. In such a scenario, the board must either lean on the management company to fix any outstanding issues or, failing that, hire a different management company that will.

Fortunately, a well-intentioned but underinformed board is usually quick to act once it understands the problem. If directors are alerted to a problem like a persistent roof leak in the community clubhouse, they will likely be genuinely shocked and appalled that they've been left in the dark about something so important and damaging. Embarrassed by their ignorance, they'll leap into action to tackle the problem directly and make lasting, meaningful change within the community. However, if the board fails to recognize and address such issues promptly, it signals a major red flag for the community's well-being and the board's commitment to effective governance.

I've built a career taking on bad boards that don't know when to let up. That said, I've found that most boards don't want a fight, which requires time and money they don't want to spend. If your request makes sense and is based on the governing documents, and if you've outlined a reasonable solution, board members are generally inclined to take the path of least resistance. But you must be proactive in enforcing your rights.

When dealing with a bad board, it's okay to show you aren't afraid of bringing that pain. As Teddy Roosevelt famously said, "Speak softly and carry a big stick." That could mean sending a polite letter pointing out the provisions of the CC&Rs that the HOA has ignored, marshaling a contingent of community members to get the pool fixed, or threatening legal action. If these personal efforts get the board to resolve the issue appropriately without a lawyer, you've saved some money and time. If they don't result in a fix, you can always bring out the big guns.

REASON #3: BAD MANAGEMENT COMPANIES

About half the bad HOA cases we get have their root cause in bad management companies.

The HOA is the legal entity that has a relationship with all the homeowners in its community. It oversees the CC&Rs and governing documents and is required to uphold the standard of care and maintenance outlined in them. The HOA itself is merely a board of directors elected by the community to act as the association's governing body. While the buck stops with the board, the board members typically don't have the time or resources to run the day-to-day of the HOA and enforce the CC&Rs. So, they contract with a management company that handles all the details—collecting dues, enforcing CC&Rs, and approving requests and work orders.

Good management companies do exist. Many management companies are skilled at what they do. Many others, however, aren't. As discussed in the previous section, things can go wrong when a bad management company drops the ball either by failing to perform its contractually obligated duties or by incorrectly performing that work.

These failures can manifest in several ways:

- Wrongfully collecting dues or misapplying fines to accounts
- Being too enthusiastic about finding and fining residents for small infractions, resulting in the harassment of some homeowners
- Padding its profit margin by subcontracting maintenance and repairs of common areas to a cheap vendor that does more harm than good

- Failing to inspect the common areas, leading to problems like significant roof leaks that result in extensive property damage for several owners in the building

These are just a few examples of how a bad management company can cause problems for you, the homeowner. Adding insult to injury, these management companies have next to no customer service and follow-up. They may ignore repeated attempts to contact them—or make it practically impossible to reach them at all. They may give incomplete or confusing information that sets you up for an infraction and fine. Or they may respond inconsistently to communications from homeowner to homeowner, demanding that one homeowner secure permission from the HOA to build an in-ground pool while telling another homeowner that such permission is not required.

RESPONDING TO A BAD MANAGEMENT COMPANY

There are several ways to address a rogue management company; most involve taking the issue directly to the board. For example, California state law allows a home-owner to hold the HOA board responsible for the conduct of its contractors. By this thinking, the management company is merely an arm of the association and not its head. Therefore, the HOA should be liable for damages caused by its contractors.

Under HOA laws like California's, even if the management company screwed up, the HOA board will be held liable. No matter how hard they might try, the board members cannot sidestep their responsibility to the homeowners. If you live in a state with similar laws governing the conduct of HOAs, your board must do the following:

- Hire effective contractors to fulfill the HOA's responsibilities
- Provide proper vetting, accountability, and oversight
- Confirm a maintenance policy or calendar with the management company

If your board fails in these duties, it is likely responsible for the consequences of that ignorance or apathy.

In such an instance, the first and best move is to call a formal meeting with your HOA board (assuming your CC&Rs allow you to do so). In that meeting, you can show the board members proof of the management company's negligence. The problems might be news to the directors, who had assumed everything was going fine. If they are operating in good faith, they will welcome this news and act swiftly—often to fire the management company and pursue damages (if that action makes good business sense).

Of course, if your board is also rotten (which we'll discuss more in the next chapter), this meeting is unlikely to be fruitful. In such a case, the board members probably already know the management company is a train wreck; they just keep paying the company out of laziness or an active lack of giving a damn about how the company's mismanagement harms their community.

SYMPTOMS OF A GREATER PROBLEM

Bad management companies *do* happen, and bad HOA boards enable them. HOA boards are composed of volunteer residents of a community, and administering a big community is a full-time job. Even if they wanted to be, three part-time board members can't be everywhere at once. They have jobs, families, and plenty to worry about with regard to their HOA responsibilities. Due to these time limitations, it makes sense to hire someone to do a good and reliable job administering the daily tasks of a community's government, just as city and state governments form different departments and hire subcontractors to fix roads and provide public services like trash collection and electricity.

But here's the rub. There's such a significant demand for management companies that even ones that do a terrible job still get hired. There isn't much competition or incentive to do an excellent job, and they can make more money by paying peanuts to inexperienced employees and cheap subcontractors. At indifferent and inept management companies, turnover is often high because no one likes to field constant complaints and abuse from disgruntled homeowners. As a result, employees at these companies often haven't been there for long and are essentially learning their roles on the job—which makes for uniformly lousy service.

The HOAs hiring these management companies may think something is better than nothing, a mediocre company is all they can afford, or the devil they know is better than the devil they don't. Or it's just that ignorance and laziness again. No one wants to fire an established company and hire and onboard a new one, especially not when all that work is unpaid time. Staying with a bad company can also stem from something less sinister but no less impactful: they don't know what makes for a good management company and have no idea how to vet one or assess its performance.

HOAs are inherently human entities, from the people they serve to the people who run them to the people they hire. Like any government, it takes a lot of diligent and conscientious humans to make them work. The members of a well-intentioned volunteer board who still haven't put all the pieces together deserve some empathy.

That said, they still must comply with the governing documents, operate in a manner consistent with applicable law, and abide by their fiduciary obligations. As the governing body of a community, the board is responsible for ensuring that its vendors and contractors serve its members according to the stipulations outlined in its governing documents. When the financial sustainability and physical health of the community are at stake, inexperience can only be an excuse for so long.

IS YOUR HOA ENGAGING IN GOOD FAITH?

As we wind down this chapter, I want to stress that not all HOAs and management companies are inept. There are some very well-run associations out there that help build thriving, active communities. A properly maintained and operated HOA preserves fair market value for properties by ensuring everyone in the community meets and complies with specific standards of maintenance and citizenship, bringing tremendous value to all.

This is the ideal—and the reason why HOAs exist in the first place. However, for too many homeowners, the ideal is not the reality. Even if you are a relatively low-key resident who tries to follow all the rules, life can throw you a curveball. You might be called away to help a sick family member for a few days and, as a result, neglect to pull your empty trash bins off the curb and back out of sight.

Unfortunately, in instances like this, the modus operandi of many bad-faith HOAs is to punish or target residents for simple infractions rather than to work jointly with them to resolve the issue. Instead of taking a constructive approach, these HOAs often choose to exert their power through harassment or excessive penalties, creating an atmosphere of fear and resentment among homeowners.

This "punish first and ask questions later" approach helps no one. All it does is set up a hostile, oppositional dynamic between the board and the community members that board was meant to serve. When you live in a community with a board operating in good faith, you'll likely smile and wave if you see a board member walking past your home. However, if your board is operating in bad faith, you'll respond with distrust and paranoia when you see a board member walking by, quickly scrambling to ensure your yard is free of infractions.

If you live in a community where it feels like your board isn't on your side, is constantly trying to find something wrong, or worse, doesn't seem to understand or care about the health and success of your community, then you've got a problem. As Americans, we pride ourselves on our independence—especially regarding the sovereignty of property ownership. When a petty regulatory body is breathing down our necks or neglecting to follow up on its public responsibilities, it can cause us endless frustration and angst.

When this frustration bubbles up, should your first reaction be to go to war with your board? Probably not, although as we'll see in the following chapters, sometimes war is inevitable. The first response should be to respond objectively and analytically. As we've seen in this chapter, most HOAs don't go bad because of bad actors but because of the genuine challenges embedded in their formation and governance. Throw in neglectful and predatory management companies, and you have a recipe for disaster.

However, these are only the functional causes of a bad HOA. At its heart, an HOA is run by and for people voluntarily. As we'll explore in the next chapter, your HOA's board of directors can fall prey to several bad actors. Therefore, it's important to understand the kinds of bad actors you may encounter in your HOA if you want to respond to them effectively.

KEY TAKEAWAYS

- There are three main reasons HOAs go bad: volunteer boards, inaction, and subpar management companies.

- Bad-faith HOAs either don't care about the personal challenges their community members face or don't understand their responsibilities in accordance with the laws and obligations that govern them.

- Some for-profit management companies are highly rated and do an excellent job servicing their clients' HOAs. Others exist only as a grift. However, because demand far exceeds supply, even poor management companies can often thrive.

"Know your enemy and know yourself, and you can fight a hundred battles without disaster."

—SUN TZU

The Usual Combatants

OP QUIZ: IS YOUR HOA'S BOARD OF DIRECTORS composed of reasonable, intelligent people?

If you picked up this book, then probably not. If you're unsure, you should have a clearer idea of how to tell by the end of this chapter—and what to do about it.

Whatever the case, as goes the quality of your board members, so goes the quality of your homeowners association. It's very rare for reasonable, intelligent people to lead an unhealthy, dysfunctional HOA. A board that understands its fiduciary obligations and takes seriously its purpose of improving its community typically functions well. Problems may arise, but they don't stay problems for long—meaning that you, the homeowner, can go about your usual business.

That said, a board full of reasonable, intelligent people can be hard to find in any industry, let alone in a voluntary HOA that offers no pay, no benefits, and no rewards save for a healthy community.

This begs the question: If not money or perks, what does a board member get out of their position?

Sometimes, motives are positive and altruistic: to give back to their community, feel purposeful, leverage a skill set, or keep busy. But sometimes motives are more sinister.

Of the HOA-related cases my team sees that escalate to the need for legal intervention, most are rooted in a conflict with bad actors on the board of directors. After all, there's a finite cast of characters generally drawn to HOA boards. Some are good, some are incompetent, and some are true villains. The bad ones each have a unique brand of chaos that sows discord within a community and impedes the mission of effective decision-making and community cohesion.

Fortunately, they can also be stopped. In this chapter, we'll identify the Usual Combatants you will likely find on your board and describe how to recognize and respond to these habitual wrongdoers. Then, for the rest of the book, we'll discuss the many avenues for amelioration available if your initial interventions prove fruitless.

But first, before we get into the negatives, let's briefly review the positives—the types of people you hope will be on your HOA board.

THE HERO

The Hero has a useful skill they want to share with the community. Maybe they are a wiz at putting together a spreadsheet, know about native plants and sustainable landscaping, have experience in real estate management, or have just retired from a position as a high-powered executive assistant and can organize the hell out of any event or unruffle the ruffliest of feathers. They know their value and can help improve the functioning of the association, and they want to take care of their fellow neighbors to ensure a happy and healthy community that maintains its property values.

Heroes, in other words, want to serve their community. They may be retirees or empty nesters, people who otherwise have spare time and energy but need a purpose or avenue to channel their desire to help others and manage a dynamic organization. A Hero can do a good job without money. Their reward is the emotional capital of service. They represent the ideal board member, and they are the golden goose of high-functioning HOAs.

That said, not all Heroes are looking for board jobs. Some are Reluctant Heroes who feel compelled to run for a board position to counterbalance the bad actors on the board. For instance, one homeowner I know (we'll call her Nancy) teamed up with a friend to run for the community's two open board positions because she was tired of constant mistreatment at the hands of the board—specifically in the form of undeserved fines. Nancy and her friend won and proceeded to abolish the many practices that had caused residents so much frustration.

Reluctant Heroes like these are motivated to do the right thing. They can't sit idle while bad board members run their community into the ground—or, in Nancy's case, make it a miserable place to live.

Unfortunately, as we'll see in the following sections, these Heroes are often the exception rather than the rule.

THE TYRANT

The Nightmare Hills community was excited to welcome Charles as the board's newest member. His appeal to the residents of Nightmare Hills was simple: prioritize efficiency and adopt a governing philosophy that would uphold current HOA standards and maintain—or increase—property values.

At first, that's exactly what Charles did. His first few years on the board were pleasantly unremarkable—no conflict, controversy, or untoward behavior. However, the more Charles became entrenched in his position, the more his true colors emerged. Where community meetings once featured open debate and a spirit of compromise, Charles now ruled over the proceedings with an iron fist, dismissing or even shouting down dissenting voices until he had his way (or even going so far as to turn off various homeowners' Zoom access when he did not like what they said).

Even worse, his decisions had become increasingly arbitrary. Gone were the well-intentioned compromises and community-first mindset he claimed to stand for. In their place was an almost fanatical focus on consolidating power and "being right." Under Charles the Tyrant's rule, the community spirit of Nightmare Hills began to crumble.

RECOGNIZING THE SIGNS OF A TYRANT

Tyrants tend to prioritize authoritarianism and control while disregarding the opinions and concerns of others. As we just saw with the story of Charles, the Tyrant takes the lead and holds on to it by shooting down any alternative opinions or objections. He's combative, keeping to a very strict binary of right and wrong—a binary in which he's always right.

Tyrants can cloak their nature when running for the board, so sometimes they may be hard to spot. But while they may act civil at first, their true colors always come out eventually.

For Wendy, a longtime resident of Nightmare Hills, the warning signs that Charles had lost the script were initially subtle. Eventually, however, she began to see a pattern of behavior that alarmed her. Here are some of the most troubling behaviors Wendy noticed. If you see any of these behavior patterns emerge in one of your board members, you too might have a Tyrant on your hands.

Limited Community Input

Tyrants often restrict homeowners' opportunities to participate in decision-making processes. They minimize or eliminate avenues for community input, creating a significant gap between the board and the residents it serves.

This can be a sometimes subtle tactic—one that Wendy didn't notice at first. However, when she began piecing a few smaller annoyances together, she realized they fit a more troubling picture:

- Community meetings became less frequent.
- Regular updates on community boards began to decrease as well.
- When the board *did* make announcements, community members were often blindsided by big decisions that they hadn't been involved in but that directly affected them.

Because of this flagrant lack of transparency, Wendy quickly grew to distrust the HOA's information about upcoming projects.

Authoritarianism

Tyrants wield authority with an iron fist, often making decisions unilaterally without seeking input from fellow board members or homeowners. They expect unwavering compliance with their directives, leaving little room for open discussion or debate and dismissing alternative viewpoints and ideas.

Authoritarian Tyrants also frequently disregard established rules and procedures. They may selectively enforce rules or manipulate processes to further their objectives, often with little regard for fairness or due process.

For instance, when the board at Nightmare Hills decided to add hardscaping and new plants to all the community's main thoroughfares, it didn't notify the community until the decision had already been made. Wendy tried to raise a voice in protest, noting how expensive the renovation was, but Charles forcefully rejected her objections and rushed the decision through the board.

Resistance to Accountability

Tyrants don't like being held accountable for their actions. They often avoid explaining their decisions, evade checks and balances, and dismiss negative outcomes and homeowner concerns as insignificant.

When Wendy raised her concerns about how the new landscaping project was halfway through its budget but only 25 percent complete, Charles quickly waved her concerns off. "They'll get to your street eventually," he said. "Our timeline just may be a bit longer."

Personal Agendas

A Tyrant's interests often supersede the community's well-being. They make decisions that primarily serve their own desires, rather than considering what is best for the homeowners. Unsurprisingly, Charles's part of the neighborhood was the first to receive its new hardscaping, while Wendy's languished in disrepair. It looked like Nightmare Hills was divided between the haves and the have-nots.

Intimidation and Bullying

Challenging a Tyrant can come at a cost. Homeowners who dare to question or oppose a Tyrant's actions may face unwarranted fines, targeted rule enforcement, or exclusion from community activities. This behavior creates a tense and hostile environment for the board and the community. In short, a Tyrant is a bully and rules the board through intimidation and dominance.

The Tyrant's primary motivation is power. Power corrupts, and absolute power corrupts absolutely, right? After Wendy made repeated attempts to request updated timetables for the community beautification project, she began to receive citations for small infractions that had never been a problem before. She was even told to take down a sculpture she'd had in her front garden for years because it "hadn't been approved" by the HOA. She was mystified by the board's behavior—and unsure what to do about it.

THE MEDDLER

Margaret was a dedicated community member eager to ensure that Nosy Neighbors Ranch remained a pristine and well-maintained haven. She had served on the board for years, and residents appreciated and welcomed her presence in many ways.

However, there was one problem: Margaret had a penchant for meddling in the personal lives of her fellow homeowners. She would snoop around the neighborhood, inserting her opinion on every design or decoration choice within the community, from the color of exterior paint to landscaping.

Some of this feedback could be attributed to doing her job. After all, most HOAs have a say in how their residents paint and landscape the exterior of their homes. The problem, in this case, was overreach: Margaret didn't follow the appropriate channels to provide feedback, and often, her meddling and nitpicking fell well outside the purview of the HOA.

Over time, Margaret's unchecked meddling spread like a virus, turning Nosy Neighbors Ranch into a hotbed of anxiety and tension. Homeowners became terrified of altering their homes, fearing their choices might run afoul of Margaret's particular sense of aesthetics. Despite her best intentions, Margaret the Meddler was putting an undue strain on her entire community.

RECOGNIZING THE SIGNS OF A MEDDLER

The Meddler has no boundaries, running around at a hundred miles an hour and putting out fires that don't exist. They overcommunicate, overexplain, and overcompensate. They are detail oriented and know the governing documents backward and forward—even if they selectively interpret those documents to suit their own perspective.

Margaret's meddling ways were already well established when a young couple named Mark and Lisa moved into Nosy Neighbors Ranch. At first, these new residents were charmed by Margaret's impromptu appearances at their door, which were seemingly a sign of neighborly goodwill. But they began to suspect something was wrong when she offered unsolicited advice about their choice of curtains, garden plants, and even the color of their baby's nursery.

When a member of your HOA board engages in unwarranted interference, as Margaret did with Mark and Lisa, it may indicate a tendency to push boundaries and disrupt the harmony of the community. While each Meddler is unique in their particular quirks and pet peeves, below are some of the most common traits of a Meddler.

Excessive Curiosity

The Meddler thrives on information; it's the social capital Margaret spends to increase her status. She's insatiably curious and devotes all her spare hours to gleaning information about her neighbors and commenting on the neighborhood's social media pages with complaints or compliments. This insatiable curiosity extends into the private lives of fellow homeowners, and she inquires about matters that do not pertain to the community's affairs.

When Mark and Lisa posted about crib recommendations on the neighborhood Facebook group, Margaret seemed overly enthusiastic about her suggestions and accompanied them with a lecture on childcare. During her frequent visits, she asked for more information on Lisa's due date and if she could help in other ways. Eventually, Mark and Lisa had had enough.

A Tendency to Micromanage

The Meddler wants to improve things and ensure everyone follows the rules, but this desire can lead to an unhealthy amount of sticking their nose in everyone's business. They want to micromanage, often extending their reach beyond their designated HOA responsibilities.

Gossiping and Spreading Rumors

The Meddler doesn't want a board position for the abstract notion of work or to protect the community; they want it because it puts them right in the middle of the community's social hub. It gives them an all-access pass to potential romantic partners, gossip, and juicy information. They get to know what everyone else is doing and to pass judgment on those things to their gaggle of hangers-on.

Excessive curiosity can lead to unintended sticky situations like gossip and rumors. The Meddler might disclose personal, privileged, or confidential information, either from the members to the board or from the board to the members. Remember, information is the Meddler's stock-in-trade. It's how they earn respect, status, and attention, but they aren't strategic about it. They may share information that can damage reputations.

Selective Enforcement

The Meddler's nature is to overreach, but while they're focused on juicy small infractions and what people are doing behind closed doors, they forget their real duties: the day-to-day governance they were elected to the board to fulfill.

Meddlers may also exhibit favoritism, enforcing rules selectively against certain homeowners based on personal biases. This unequal treatment can poison the atmosphere within the entire community.

Personal Agendas

Hidden agendas or personal vendettas may underlie a Meddler's actions, resulting in decisions that do not serve the best interests of the community as a whole. They can't help but interject their opinion and advice into others' lives, and that engagement energizes them, whether or not those interjections are welcome or helpful. They may go outside their authority as a board member to investigate potential problems or infractions that aren't visible or apparent.

One Sunday morning, Lisa opened her door to find Margaret there with a list of food items. "I'm here to help you clean out your pantry," she declared. "These are all the things pregnant women with complications like you shouldn't be eating." Lisa had to bite her tongue. How had Margaret known about her health issues? Had Mark told her?

Lisa wanted to shut the door in Margaret's face, but she'd heard from other neighbors who'd stood up to Margaret, and that's when the real trouble started. One neighbor, for instance, began receiving regular infractions for not cleaning the outside of her mailbox! Reluctantly, Lisa let Margaret in and spent a whole afternoon with her, throwing out hundreds of dollars' worth of food.

THE FOOL

Edward ran for Shoddy Hollow's HOA board because he thought it would be cool. He'd get to hang out with his golf buddies in the community clubhouse and raise his social status. Edward liked people, after all. When he was finally elected, he couldn't have been happier with the result.

However, to Shoddy Hollow residents Amanda and Michael, Edward was like a kid learning to play Monopoly for the first time: he's not trying to lose, but he doesn't know better. Unlike a kid and a board game, where the only consequence is a parent wanting to pull their hair out, mistakes while serving on an HOA board impact real people's lives.

All evidence pointed to the same inevitable conclusion: Shoddy Hollow was suffering at the hands of a Fool. Here's how Amanda and Michael discovered him.

RECOGNIZING THE SIGNS OF A FOOL

The Fool doesn't realize they're taking control of millions of dollars' worth of real estate and the lives of the people who bought that real estate. They don't take their responsibilities seriously, don't understand what they're doing, and don't care. They take the path of least resistance to address problems and view every situation through a cookie-cutter lens, not thinking about how their actions might impact others.

A subset of the Fool is the Altruistic Fool, who wants to get on the board to make change and do right by the community they love. They want to get out there and paint that faded fence, unaware that doing so requires them to run that proposed task and its expense through a committee to approve the budget, the schedule, and the contractors— contractors who need to be bonded and licensed with the proper permits.

The other subset of Fool is the Old-Timer. An Old-Timer has been on the board through many election cycles. Maybe they've been on the board for decades. And how they ran the board on day one is how they run the board now. They still contract with the landscape company that cut the grass when the community was first built, and they golf with the owner on the weekends, even though the prices have increased fourfold since then. The Old-Timer is on the board because they don't know what else to do and are not interested in what newer homeowners want or need. They have no interest in learning about current real estate trends and this new generation of home buyers. They're content to let the management company and the other board members handle the day-to-day, trusting they are handling things appropriately. The Old-Timer doesn't want to fight with anyone and avoids confrontation and complaints like the plague, hoping they will disappear.

Below are some typical characteristics of a Fool.

Lack of Understanding of Governing Documents
Fools demonstrate a limited grasp of the HOA's governing documents. To them, bylaws, rules, and regulations are akin to a foreign language. A Fool generally hasn't even read the governing documents they're supposed to uphold. If they do try to read those, they don't know how to parse the legalese.

When Amanda and Michael asked about the blight of dying trees from recent droughts and the plan to replace them with more drought-resistant species, Edward met them with a blank stare. He had no idea it was part of his responsibility to maintain the landscaping of common areas. This raised an important question: If Edward and the rest of the board didn't understand the HOA's governing documents, how could they make informed decisions aligned with the community guidelines and fulfill their mandate as board members?

Poor Communication Skills

Effective communication is paramount, but Fools encounter challenges in conveying messages effectively. Consequently, misunderstandings, confusion, and strained community relations may ensue.

Amanda and Michael needed clarification about water restrictions in the summer. The governing documents stated the grass had to be green and well maintained, but the city mandated only semiweekly watering. Michael didn't want to get a hefty fine from the city and wanted to do his part to conserve water, but he also didn't want to run afoul of the HOA's governing documents. When he confronted Edward with this contradiction, Edward told him to follow the city ordinance on water restrictions. "But that means brown lawns," Michael said. "Is that okay?" Another blank stare.

A month later, after Michael allowed the lawn to go brown, he and Amanda were fined for not maintaining their grass. Thanks to Edward's lack of awareness and non-committal responses, Michael now had a bigger problem on his hands.

Inability to Fulfill Board Responsibilities

Fools often lack the skills to run an HOA, such as creating and understanding contracts for management and maintenance companies. They don't know how to budget or balance the books. They're ignorant of third-party resources that could help streamline daily tasks like collecting dues. Maintenance tasks in common areas don't get done well or at all. Established decision-making and dispute-resolution rules are ignored, resulting in inconsistent governance and exposing the HOA to potential legal consequences.

In the few months they had lived in Shoddy Hollow, Amanda and Michael witnessed a striking pattern of ineptitude. Edward made haphazard budgetary decisions. For instance, in the middle of the summer, he contracted a team to plant new, young trees to replace the dead ones, but he failed to repair and set up the irrigation system to keep them watered. As a result, the trees all died, and the community's money dried up. There was no funding left to maintain the neglected community areas like the pool and clubhouse. What was the point of paying dues if that money didn't go anywhere useful?

Resistance to Learning

Fools are reluctant to acquire new knowledge or engage in training sessions that could enhance their understanding of HOA management, legal obligations, and community governance.

When Amanda and Michael asked what the management company's schedule looked like for the common areas or who was supposed to be watering the baby trees, Edward didn't know. "Didn't the landscaper advise when would be the best time to plant young trees and what their care should be?" Amanda asked.

"I don't need a landscaper to tell me how to plant a tree. You just dig a hole and stick it in the ground. It isn't rocket science," Edward shrugged. "The trees are probably losing their leaves for the fall."

"But it's August," Amanda protested.

Cue another blank stare.

Inconsistent Decision-Making

Incompetent board members often make decisions incoherently or inconsistently, confusing homeowners and eroding the board's credibility.

When Amanda and Michael wanted to install an in-ground pool, just like their neighbor had the month prior, the board rejected their application even though it proposed similar plans. "But why? Other community members had the same plans," Michael asked.

"The plans didn't meet the criteria for approval," Edward replied.

However, when Michael asked for those criteria, Edward couldn't furnish them or provide feedback on correcting the request. A month later, when Michael submitted almost the exact same plans, the pool was approved.

THE SELF-DEALER

Daniel knew what he was doing was wrong. He knew it was unethical to manipulate HOA contracts in a way that directly benefited him. But, he reasoned, no one had caught him yet, so why should he stop?

Such is the mindset of the chronic Self-Dealer. Within the community, Self-Dealers are masters at keeping up appearances, projecting the image of a diligent and responsible steward of their HOA. Behind closed doors, however, their actions paint a different picture. For years, Daniel had been manipulating business deals with the HOA for his financial benefit, awarding contracts to companies in which he had a hidden stake and funneling funds meant for community improvement into his own pockets.

Daniel had told himself he'd only engage in these self-dealing activities once or twice, and then he would stop. But the temptation proved too great. As he grew more confident, he also grew more careless. Maintenance and community improvement projects were left half-finished,

HOA fees and fines skyrocketed, and the Sleepy Sheep Estates community began to suspect something wasn't right. All evidence pointed to Daniel, but how could anyone know for sure?

RECOGNIZING THE SIGNS OF A SELF-DEALER

The Self-Dealer is the most dangerous bad actor. The Tyrant may act selfishly, but since they don't see their actions as wrong, they rarely try to hide their personality. But the Self-Dealer is a con artist—a true criminal. All they want is money, and their motive for being elected to the board tends to be purely economic. In some cases, they may get elected for other reasons, realize the board is weak, and take advantage of the chaos.

The Self-Dealer loves the more visible bad actors, like the Tyrant and Meddler, because those members serve as a shield as they attract all the community's attention. The Self-Dealer knows the system and how to play it; all they need is access and someone looking the other way. Like a chameleon, they often present well, get along with everyone, and seem to follow all the rules.

Kat and Kendrick moved into Sleepy Sheep Estates, dreaming of raising their family in this once-thriving community. As the problems mounted, however, they began to wonder if they'd made the right choice. All around them, they could see that something wasn't quite right with the board, but often, specific problems proved difficult to pinpoint.

As they worked with other community members to piece together the story, Kat and Kendrick recognized the following issues.

Financial Gain

Self-Dealers consistently make decisions that serve their personal financial interests or business endeavors, even if those conflict with what's good for the community. On the back end, the Self-Dealer siphons money off the association's reserves or gets kickbacks from friends. They have no desire to benefit anyone other than themselves. Sometimes, the Self-Dealer's financial shenanigans are just blatant. Daniel literally wrote checks to himself for "expenses."

Alarm bells sounded in Kat and Kendrick's heads when a rolling notice went around the neighborhood giving all homeowners ninety days to replace their fences, even though their existing fences were only five years old. Why this added onus on homeowners? Let's continue.

Conflict of Interest

There might be some interesting personal connections between the Self-Dealer and all the contractors hired to fulfill lucrative new project contracts. The Self-Dealer may even advocate for weird spending projects at a higher-than-market rate. Suppose the HOA consistently approves the most expensive project bid, and the Self-Dealer always gives overzealous reasons why the most expensive option is better and why this seemingly incompetent vendor should be kept—or acts very protective of certain contractor relationships. In that case, they might be getting kickbacks from the contractors.

Kat and Kendrick's suspicions deepened when a high-priced contractor was named as the one who should replace the fences "to maintain community visual standards," even though the CC&Rs clearly stated a range of fence options and didn't restrict third-party contractors. Digging deeper, Kat found that Daniel's cousin, Vinny, owned the fencing company.

Lack of Transparency and Accountability

When a Self-Dealer is at work, a lot of money goes out the door, but not much value is added to the community. The HOA has constant money issues and depleted reserves, and it has no idea how those problems came to be. This is because the Self-Dealer has cooked the books, entering incorrect numbers to hide where the money truly goes. They also might be the first to explain away financial discrepancies or seem unconcerned about them.

The Self-Dealer will do anything to avoid their cover being blown and their prize goose plucked from under them. They avoid transparency, audits, and disclosing their affiliations, because they don't want others to discover what they're up to. The more a Self-Dealer manipulates information and decision-making processes to safeguard their interests, the more their obfuscation becomes evident.

Abuse of Power

Exploiting their position, Self-Dealers enjoy privileges beyond the reach of other homeowners, including preferential treatment in rule enforcement or exclusive access to community amenities. They often negotiate for personal compensation or perks that far exceed what is equitable or customary for their role on the board, raising concerns of impropriety.

RESPONDING TO THE USUAL COMBATANTS

Now that you understand more about the Usual Combatants you're likely to encounter on your board, the big question is: What do you do about it?

Engaging a lawyer is always an option, but in most cases, it should be your last option. Here are some other tactics to start with instead.

DOCUMENT EVERYTHING
Best for: Tyrants, Meddlers, Self-Dealers

Be careful what you say in front of Tyrants or Meddlers, as everything you say can and will be used against you in the HOA court of public opinion.

Because of these behaviors, one of the smartest things you can do when encountering a Tyrant or a Meddler is to document everything. Don't call them out in meetings (unless you legally record the conversation). Instead, communicate through formal emails or letters. Make copies of everything you send, including their responses. If they reach out to you in person or via phone, make notes of your encounter immediately afterward.

Similarly, if you suspect a Self-Dealer, the best thing you can do is gather evidence to support your claims. This may involve researching contracts, financial records, and related parties. If you don't yet have the legal evidence, just suspicions, then take these suspicions to the board without pointing a finger at any one director. This information is best presented to the whole board at once. Chances are the rest of the board is not involved with the Self-Dealer's machinations and will take action, maybe starting an internal investigation with their attorney to follow the money.

ENGAGE THE COMMUNITY
Best for: Tyrants, Meddlers, Fools, Self-Dealers

If you suspect you're dealing with one of the Usual Combatants, the best way to confirm your suspicions is to share your concerns with your neighbors. One of the most effective approaches is to attend HOA meetings and encourage open discussion about your coalition's concerns. After all, there is strength in numbers. Here's what might happen when you do:

- The Tyrant or the Meddler might push back at first. However, once they've lost their power, many will choose to surrender their position on the board entirely, seeing that they can no longer wield their influence.

- The Self-Dealer will realize they've been smoked out and give in. Sure, they might raise a stink, accusing others in the community of harassment or discrimination, but it will all be bluster. And besides, since you've documented everything, you're ready to push back against any false accusations.

- The Fool will likely be embarrassed when they see the impact of their incompetence on the community. Be gentle but firm, allowing them opportunities to change their ways.

Like any of these suggestions, this tactic isn't foolproof, and confronting these bad actors will take some bravery. However, I've found that direct engagement with your community is a strong means of avoiding unnecessary escalation.

PLAY TO THEIR EGO
Best for: Tyrants, Meddlers

Instead of being strong like stone, be strong like water. Listen attentively to what the Combatant in front of you has to say, frame your talking points in a way that's flattering to them, and allow them to feel heroic—even while you're getting your way. For instance, if Charles the Tyrant still hasn't finished the beautification project, flatter him into it. "You did a great job with the first area of the neighborhood," you might say. "In your opinion, what will it take to finish the rest?"

DIRECT COMMUNICATION
Best for: Meddlers, Fools

Most of us don't enjoy confrontation. However, to foster a healthy community, it is crucial to emphasize clear communication, adherence to community guidelines, and a steadfast commitment to fair governance.

Precision counts with Meddlers and Fools, and since they intend to do good, so does a little compassion. Sometimes, sitting down and politely explaining and identifying problems and code violations can work. A certain amount of confidence—of being the calm adult in the room—can make the difference.

With a Meddler, this is also a chance to establish better boundaries. They want to be right up close, while everyone else wants them at arm's length to maintain separation between the roles of friend and board director. Politely but firmly communicate your boundaries and state that unsolicited sharing, help, and advice outside the purview of the HOA is unwelcome. If there is a way they can better help you *within* the purview of the HOA, state that as well.

EDUCATION AND TRAINING
Best for: Fools

Education—presented politely, simply, and in a way that doesn't *make* someone feel like a Fool—is usually the best course of action. Show the Fool a path forward. Suggest or provide educational resources and training opportunities for the board member to improve their knowledge and skills. If the association already contracts with a competent corporate attorney or management company, the Fool may learn enough on the fly to make it work.

Once the Fool is no longer foolish, they'll want to do right by you to make up for the pain caused by their ignorance. In moments like these, your best move is to work hand in hand with the board as a collaborative problem solver. We've seen Fools turn it around within a year of being elected and become quite good at their duties. But if the Fool doesn't have those resources or is ignorant of how to leverage them, or if the management company or subcontractors are already corrupted, there may be no hope of improvement.

ESTABLISH OVERSIGHT
Best for: Tyrants, Self-Dealers

Establish mechanisms for oversight, transparency, and conflict-of-interest mitigation within the HOA. Ensure that legal and ethical standards are the guiding principles in promoting fair and just community governance. Insist on full disclosure of contracts, financial statements, and potential conflicts of interest.

ENGAGE A LAWYER
Best for: Tyrants, Meddlers, Fools, Self-Dealers

When all else fails, engage a lawyer. We'll talk more about this in Chapter 7, but typically, your goal isn't to go to court; it's to force action. For their own reasons, Tyrants, Meddlers, Fools, and Self-Dealers all present obstacles to action. A lawyer can help overcome those obstacles.

Of the Usual Combatants, Self-Dealers are typically the only ones exposing themselves to any personal legal peril, even though, in practice, they're rarely prosecuted for whatever small-time fraud they might commit. Sometimes, a board's attorneys might sue in civil court to recover any stolen funds, but otherwise, the most typical consequence is that the Self-Dealer gets kicked off the board and departs the community in shame.

EFFECTS OF COMBATANTS ON THE DNA OF A BOARD

Now that you can recognize HOA bad actors, let's discuss how they affect a board's DNA, the basic components that allow it to function.

Imagine that your HOA board has five members. Four are Heroes who are good at what they do. When a Meddler is elected to the fifth spot, the other directors recognize the trouble immediately. More importantly, they know how to neutralize the threat of the Meddler's more damaging habits, such as redirecting meetings away from gossip. The board might even bring in corporate counsel to talk to the Meddler, explaining what confidentiality really means and the potential consequences for breaking it.

A high-functioning board with good DNA will be mostly immune to one bad actor. However, a board with weaker DNA may allow a stronger bad actor to come in and take over.

Bad actors are like viruses. Given a weak system, they can overcome defenses and multiply. A Meddler can turn on their fellow "friends" on the board and get them ousted. A Tyrant can outmuscle well-intentioned but nonconfrontational incumbents who thought introducing a "strong man" figure to get those dues in on time was a good idea. Once the board is infected, corruption spreads to the community, and people start feeling the pain—in ways that seem small at first but gradually build over time.

When an HOA goes bad, it's typically because a bad actor or two, like a rotten apple, has spoiled the whole barrel. The HOA as an entity is neutral. What makes an HOA effective or ineffective is the people who update, enforce, and execute its governing documents. If the HOA works, it's because of the humans who run it. If it's not good, it's also because of the humans who run it—or fail to run it.

Whichever types of board members you encounter at your HOA, it's important to remain respectful and professional in your interactions with HOA members, even if you strongly disagree with their actions. Open and constructive communication, along with the support of other homeowners, can often lead to positive resolutions.

If you are unsure how to contextualize or voice a particular problem, consult your HOA's governing documents for specific procedures and guidelines for addressing community conflicts and concerns.

And remember: a board is a collection of people, not a monster. When you know the people who make up your board, you also understand where and how to focus your energy. That knowledge turns you from a victim running from a monster you can't see into a warrior who knows their enemy. And that's a recipe for success—by getting the Usual Combatants to act positively, voting them off the board, or screening new candidates more diligently.

If you can recognize the type of bad actor you're dealing with, that knowledge will strengthen your position to resolve any dispute that may arise. Knowing who you're dealing with gives you a combat advantage, allowing you to strategize the best way forward in a more sophisticated way. Instead of complaining broadly that "the board is making my life a nightmare," you understand where and how to focus your concerns.

Now that you know who you're up against, it's time to develop a strategy for actually winning, and that starts with something I call issue spotting.

KEY TAKEAWAYS

- You may encounter myriad issues as a member of an HOA. Many of these issues aren't due to the nature of your HOA's bylaws but rather the malicious, overzealous, or incompetent behavior of human actors.

- It can often feel like these bad actors are out to get you or intentionally mean you harm. However, they're often overinvested in their roles, unqualified for the job, or focused more on their own self-interest.

- As you will see in later chapters, there are many possible channels to formally address your concerns. However, for most challenges, the logical first step is to confront the bad actor or raise your concerns within the community.

"To find a solution, you must first recognize the problem."

— UNKNOWN

Issue Spotting

Common Association Nightmares

I N CHAPTER 2, I INTRODUCED YOU TO FRANK, WHO had just purchased a very nice home next to a greenbelt. A popular common area in the community, the greenbelt is full of trees, shrubs, gravel trails with benches here and there, and a good-sized dog park tucked into the southeast corner.

Every morning, Frank takes his dog for a jog down the trail, stopping at the dog park for a fifteen-minute rest before heading home. This routine keeps Frank active and Mr. Puppers happy. While living in the neighborhood, he's really come to appreciate this space.

Lately, though, he's noticed that the greenbelt has lost its luster. The doggy pickup station used to be regularly stocked with trash bags. These days, it's regularly empty. Even worse, litter has begun to accumulate on the trail. And something seems wrong with the French drainage system. It used to deposit all the rainwater into a nearby creek. Now, it overflows onto the trail, making some parts impassable after an overnight rain. The HOA is responsible for the proper upkeep of each of these issues. To Frank's dismay, the board has clearly been neglectful.

One day, the old drainage system gives up the ghost and stops working completely. A puddle begins to form in Frank's yard. Frank promptly takes a photo of the drainage issue and sends it to the board on May 5 with a note saying, "I noticed this drainage issue today. Please have maintenance repair the greenbelt's French drain, the ill-kept trail, and the dog park. They're becoming hazards to public safety and property and decreasing the value of this amenity and the community at large."

No reply.

In a well-functioning HOA, the problem could stop here. The board would hire a contractor ASAP to fix the French drain, shore up the trail, and remove trail debris, and the management company would add restocking and emptying the dog trash to its weekly list of to-dos.

But no such luck for Frank. As he tries to weather the late spring rains, his nightmare worsens.

Frank is not alone in his frustration. We've heard versions of this story many times before.

A broken drain, an ill-kept trail, or a leaky roof in your condo are all symptoms of a broken system. It is important to identify and document these symptoms as soon as you've identified them. If you're considering partnering with a lawyer, digging deeper first is useful. *Why* does this problem exist? What is the root cause of the symptoms you're seeing?

In the chapter ahead, you'll learn how to turn your attention from symptom spotting to *issue spotting*. To understand what I mean by issue spotting, take a toothache. "My God, I have a toothache!" you might say. "Make it stop!" But the dentist doesn't wave a magic wand and make everything better. Instead, they do a few tests. They take an X-ray. They make you bite on a plastic stick. They subject your tooth to something cold. All these tests are to see what the root cause is. Do you have a fracture that needs a crown? Do you have a cavity that requires a filling? A bad nerve that needs a root canal?

While they're poking around in your mouth, they'll ask you a series of questions: "When did the pain start? How bad is it? Does it come and go or get worse in certain situations?" These details help them diagnose the issue and pinpoint a specific solution.

Such is the case with your HOA. They're the patient, and you're the dentist. Your job is to diagnose the problem and give it a specific, objective name—like "harassment," "negligence," or one of the many other issues we'll discuss in this chapter. After all, once you recognize the root cause of your nightmare, you can begin to wake up from it.

HARASSMENT

Homeowners association harassment is a form of unwanted, unwarranted, and persistent conduct directed toward an individual or group of homeowners within the confines of an HOA.

Such harassment within an HOA can stem from personal disputes, disagreements over association policies, or manipulation at the hands of a Self-Dealer. The repercussions of such behavior extend beyond individual grievances, negatively impacting the overall well-being and quality of life of those subjected to the harassment and creating an environment of tension and discomfort within the community.

Crucially, homeowners association harassment can take diverse forms and vary in severity. It can take the form of verbal, written, or electronic communication and include intimidation, threats, coercion, or any conduct that fosters a hostile environment for the targeted homeowners. Harassment often transcends the boundaries of normal disagreements and conflicts, evolving into a sustained pattern of conduct that inflicts distress upon the targeted individual(s).

Some common forms of harassment include the following:

- Excessive and unjust fines
- Continuous unfounded complaints
- Interference with property usage
- Social exclusion
- Physical, verbal, and written threats

Take the case of Maggie, a diligent homeowner dedicated to maintaining her property according to the guidelines set forth by the Crumbling Foundation Estates Homeowners Association. The trouble begins innocently enough—a garden gnome left to dry on the front walk after being repainted, a garbage bin left out too long—minor infractions that should, at most, only get her a friendly reminder to put her stuff away.

However, Maggie regularly receives hefty fines for each perceived violation. The penalties, disproportionate to the nature of the infractions, start piling up, creating a financial burden for Maggie and her family. She perceives this pattern of excessive fines as a punitive onslaught rather than a constructive effort to maintain community standards. After a few months of this behavior, Maggie can't help but wonder: Who did she piss off to receive such treatment?

SELECTIVE ENFORCEMENT

Selective enforcement is a close relative of harassment. It occurs when a specific homeowner or cohort experiences more enforcement of rules, regulations, and policies than other community members. In short, rules are repeatedly applied differently to one person than another. Residents may see the HOA's actions as arbitrary or influenced by factors unrelated to the CC&Rs, which may create a perception among homeowners of unequal treatment, favoritism, and discrimination.

PREFERENTIAL TREATMENT

Preferential treatment is the opposite of selective enforcement: a homeowner or group of homeowners is treated better than everyone else when it comes to community rules, regulations, and policies. Preferential treatment can manifest in various ways, including selectively overlooking rule violations, providing exemptions, or offering exclusive benefits to particular residents. Like selective enforcement, preferential treatment may also result in tension caused by perceived favoritism and bias, as the HOA displays inconsistency in its decision-making and enforcement practices.

For instance, Mary, an avid gardener, found herself in a unique position. As the HOA president's confidante, her eccentric landscaping endeavors escaped the same scrutiny that befell other homeowners. She got to keep her lawn gnomes. She got to plant a garish trellis that soon dripped with invasive English ivy, a plant that did not fit the "native only" stipulations of the CC&Rs. While other residents faced stringent assessments of their landscaping choices, Mary's flourishing flower beds and artistic hardscaping received approval and praise. The favoritism became increasingly apparent as Mary's projects consistently sailed through the approval process without the same level of scrutiny experienced by her neighbors. Community meetings, once marked by camaraderie, now echoed with concerns about fairness and equal application of the rules.

FAILURES TO MAINTAIN AND/OR REPAIR

General maintenance contributes to the physical preservation of the community and its sense of pride, unity, and overall satisfaction. Therefore, HOAs must repair and maintain the common areas collectively owned by all residents, such as parks, walkways, landscaping, recreational facilities, and gates.

If they fail to do so, this deficiency can have a cascading impact of bad outcomes, including degradation of community amenities, actual damage to real and personal property, and a reduction in curb appeal, all of which can contribute to property devaluation. Failures to maintain and/or repair can sometimes be small, like not catching a leaky irrigation system that creates a soggy puddle. These failures can also be significant, resulting in damage to homes.

Take this illustration. In Steep Grade Meadows, a slope behind the Harrison residence had been subject to erosion from uncontrolled runoff for years. As part of the greenbelt, this slope fell under the HOA's responsibility to maintain. One day, the hill, stripped of its vegetation and full of gullies, crumbled during heavy rain, sending a cascade of mud and debris crashing into the back of the Harrison property.

Fortunately, everyone was okay. But the problems weren't over. The Johnsons' house, perched near the top of the slope, saw its foundation severely weakened due to the mudslide. As a result, what should have been a small land-scaping repair now jeopardized two properties and would require an expensive retaining wall to fix.

NEGLIGENCE

The paramount objective of an HOA is to safeguard the well-being, safety, and overall satisfaction of the community it governs. Failure to keep the community safe may mean the HOA is negligent. Negligence is characterized by a notable deficiency or omission in fulfilling duties, responsibilities, and obligations incumbent upon the HOA. The HOA's lack of care and diligence means it has failed to govern properly.

Instances of negligence can take various forms, such as the failures to maintain and repair we saw in the previous section, a failure to enforce rules and regulations, or failure to respond to the concerns raised by residents.

Some forms of negligence include:

- Inadequate security measures
- Disregard for landscaping (also a form of failure to maintain)
- Failure to address nuisance complaints
- Failure to communicate in an accessible and timely manner
- Financial mismanagement

To give an example, the Swamp Rot Springs Homeowners Association was entrusted with fostering open communication and addressing residents' concerns. However, when homeowner Alex encountered some friction with his HOA over some vaguely worded property-maintenance guidelines, his requests for guidance from the HOA were brushed aside. He wasn't even sure if he was sending his questions to the right place or person.

With no official response, Alex grappled with these mounting stressors. The vague policy changes came from out of nowhere, without consultation or notification of the community. Alex felt abandoned by the very organization meant to protect his interests.

ELECTION FRAUD

Election fraud works the same way within a homeowners association as in a government election. It is characterized by deceptive or manipulative practices that seek to compromise the fairness and integrity of the election process, thereby undermining the democratic principles upon which the association operates. Such actions can have far-reaching consequences, significantly impacting the association's governance and community cohesion.

The various forms of election fraud within a homeowners association include the following:

- Vote tampering
- Coercion or intimidation
- Misinformation campaigns
- Unauthorized voter registration or removal
- Impersonation
- Bribery

Below are some explanations of terms that may be less intuitive or familiar.

In the case of *unauthorized voter removal*, we once became aware of an insider with access to the voter registration list who surreptitiously removed several homeowners known to support a particular candidate. This same individual then allowed someone else who did not qualify as a community resident or head of household to register to vote. This unauthorized manipulation altered the electorate's composition, skewing potential voters in favor of the candidate of that bad actor's choice.

Unauthorized voter registration is similar to, but slightly different from, *impersonation*. The latter describes a person claiming to be someone they are not. For example, a homeowner's daughter claimed to be the mother who actually held the deed to the home within the HOA.

ABUSE BY ARCHITECTURAL CONTROL COMMITTEES

An architectural control committee (ACC) evaluates, approves, or rejects homeowners' requests for architectural alterations to their properties. Outwardly visible elements—such as garden beds, outbuildings, patio spaces, and changes to paint color or front facade—are usually of most concern. If the ACC engages in inequitable, capricious, or discriminatory decision-making when approving or rejecting such requests, the issue is considered ACC abuse.

After a homeowner submits an application for architectural improvement, ACC abuses can take several forms:

- Conflict of interest or bias in the decision-making process that results in selective enforcement or preferential treatment

- Failure to document, communicate, or explain decisions with homeowners
- Arbitrary rejections of requests
- Retaliation
- Failure to follow the standard decision-making process
- Failure to follow architectural guidelines consistently

These abuses can get muddy and often overlap, so let's look at a more detailed scenario.

Robert decides to build a covered patio in his backyard. He diligently reviews the HOA's architectural guidelines, including specific patio size, materials, and design requirements. He submits a carefully prepared application to the ACC, including detailed plans and specifications that adhere to the HOA's guidelines. He is confident that his proposed patio design complies with the CC&Rs and that his request will be granted.

However, when the ACC reviews Robert's application, the members apply inconsistent standards:

- **Excessive Demands.** The ACC members demand multiple changes and modifications to Robert's proposed patio design without valid reasons or clear justification. They require him to use a specific type of roofing material, even though the guidelines allow for various options. They also insist on reducing the patio's size, despite approving larger patios for other homeowners in recent applications.

- **Delayed Responses**. The ACC takes an unusually long time to respond to Robert's inquiries and requests for clarification, provides vague feedback, and does not offer specific reasons for objections and requested changes.

- **Inconsistent Documentation and Enforcement**. Robert notices that the ACC's approval letters for other homeowners' projects contain fewer conditions than the extensive list of demands outlined in his approval letter.

- **Lack of Transparency**. When Robert points out the inconsistencies and asks the ACC members to explain their demands clearly, they do not respond.

In this example, the ACC's inconsistent adherence to its rules and regulations becomes evident through its selective enforcement and excessive demands for Robert. This inconsistency frustrates Robert and raises concerns about the fairness of the ACC's decision-making process within the HOA, leading to another HOA nightmare. But now Robert is armed with a label for this nightmare and can start digging for the objective cause that he can take to court.

FROM SPOTTING ISSUES
TO CAUSE OF ACTION

You can approach the situation from a more elevated, informed perspective when you have a thirty-thousand-foot view of the common problems you and your neighbors are experiencing within your HOA. In this way, you're focused on finding the pattern so that the problem isn't just about you but rather how the current environment affects everyone.

If you start by being reactionary—"My God, this is a nightmare! Make it stop!"—that's okay, but your emotions are a symptom of the problem, not the cause. Without precision and specific physical evidence you can point to, your case won't succeed.

What you want to do is frame the problem calmly and rationally. Admittedly, this is difficult when you feel like ripping someone's head off because your yard is under six inches of storm runoff. But remember, the problem isn't the runoff in your yard. The problem is that the governing documents say the HOA is responsible for maintaining the French drain that has ceased functioning.

The specific problem from a legal standpoint is a breach of contract. That's the cause of action. That's what the board needs to hear to understand your pain.

And that's what we'll discuss in the next chapter.

KEY TAKEAWAYS

- Emotional reactions are okay, but they don't win cases. Objectivity is key to winning.

- To build a successful case against your HOA, you must move from living in a nightmare to observing your situation objectively. See the bigger picture and understand the bigger cause of action leading to your problems.

- Once you begin to notice issues in your HOA, document everything. If the issue continues to spiral, this documentation will be useful evidence in building your case against the HOA.

"Precision is the difference between a warrior and a mere fighter."

–UNKNOWN

Your Ammunition

Common Causes of Action

VERY TIME IT RAINS, ALL THE RUNOFF FROM THE clogged greenbelt drain now dumps into Frank's yard—including rubbish and leaf litter—which flows downhill to his house and builds up at his foundation. It's bad enough that Frank must constantly deal with unsightly and unsanitary piles of mulch and soggy litter. It's worse that this runoff is causing serious damage to his home.

The persistent standing water threatens to erode Frank's foundation and is starting to cause wood rot along the bottom edge of the house's siding. The wood rot, in turn, could attract termites and carpenter ants, which would endanger the integrity of Frank's entire house. Frank dutifully documents the flooding on May 20, June 1, June 10, and July 5 and requests repairs to the greenbelt. Still, nothing happens.

Frank is in a living nightmare. And he's pissed.

Of course, the term "nightmare" is subjective. It's different for everyone and doesn't put a metric on the problem. A leaky condo ceiling is a nightmare, sure, but is it just a water spot or is it a deluge that damages your paint, floors, and electrical? Is it a danger to other units? The whole building? How much money is it costing you? For how long? Where does the water seem to be coming from, and why is it the HOA's responsibility to fix it?

In your pursuit of justice against a troublesome homeowners association, it's crucial to grasp the fundamental concept that underpins every legal battle: the cause of action. This goes beyond the issue and gets into the actual language that may appear in a legal action. For instance, Frank's issue is runoff and damage to his house as a result of a broken French drain. The cause of action, however, is negligence—in this case, failure to maintain community space.

Whatever issue you're experiencing, there is likely a corresponding cause of action. This cause of action forms the cornerstone upon which to build your legal case, providing the precise language needed to seek accountability from your HOA. In this chapter, we'll explore the most common causes of action as you prepare to go to war with your HOA.

WHAT IS A CAUSE OF ACTION?

A **cause of action** refers to the specific legal basis or grounds for bringing a lawsuit. It includes the facts that give rise to a legal right and allows a party to seek a remedy in court. Lawyers will analyze one or more potential causes of action to determine whether a client has a valid case. They look for evidence, the legal elements that make up a cause of action, and legal grounds to support the claim before deciding whether to pursue a lawsuit. This cause is different from the issue a homeowner might start with. For instance, "Someone's not maintaining the common area" is not a cause of action. It's just a problem. However, "The continued leak from an unrepaired roof violates Section 3.14 of the CC&Rs related to building maintenance of common areas" is *likely* a cause of action. (It could be a breach of contract claim, a negligence claim, or something else.)

This distinction is important. For a problem to become worthy of legal action, you must be able to argue that the issue you're experiencing directly ties to a potential cause of action. Merely disliking something doesn't hold water, at least not in a legal sense. You may not like the trees the HOA planted by the community entrance, for instance—but if the trees are approved species within the CC&Rs and bylaws, and if they aren't causing your property any harm, then you likely have no basis to take legal action.

When a homeowner comes to us with an issue, we first try to establish a cause of action—to separate the personal problem from the legal problem, the symptom from the disease. By connecting an issue directly to one or more causes of action, we can establish a legal basis for a complaint. In Frank's case, we would work to identify why his issue with the unmaintained common area is a legitimate *legal* problem. Most likely, it's a breach of the association's CC&Rs (or breach of contract), which state that the HOA is responsible for maintaining common areas. This responsibility is known as a *contractual obligation*, something the board must do to remain in compliance with the governing documents.

Whatever the precise cause of action, the bottom line is this: the better you understand causes of action, the more leverage you will have when taking on a bad HOA or, if it comes to it, explaining to a lawyer what you are experiencing in an elevated manner.

So, let's build your knowledge. In the following sections, we'll explore the elements that typically need to be satisfied to establish a valid cause of action. Think of these elements as the pieces of a legal puzzle that must be meticulously assembled to construct a persuasive narrative within the courtroom. Each cause of action is akin to a legal fingerprint, with its distinct features and standards of proof. As the aggrieved party, you must identify and articulate these elements and bolster your claims with compelling evidence that supports your case.

As you read this chapter, here are a few things to keep in mind:

- Since jurisdictions vary dramatically when it comes to the elements needed to satisfy causes of action, this section is general in nature and meant to provide a general idea of what you should look for. If and when you are ready to escalate, you can speak with your lawyer about the specifics of your local jurisdiction.

- Each state or individual community may use slightly different terms when issue spotting or finding causes of action. For example, someone may use the word *covenant* instead of *contract*. However, the basic concepts remain the same no matter where you live or which HOA you're dealing with. Here, I'm using the common terms applicable in the states where my firm operates.

- These causes of action are defined within the context of a general HOA lawsuit. However, other types of lawsuits have different definitions and requirements for establishing a cause of action.

- Finally, your ability to hold your HOA accountable for any of the following causes of action often comes down to causation. In other words, you must demonstrate a direct link between the HOA's misconduct and the harm or damage you suffered—i.e., you must be able to show that the HOA caused you harm.

With these clarifications out of the way, let's explore the most common causes of action.

NEGLIGENCE

A negligent HOA has failed to meet the standard of care in the management, maintenance, or operation of the community, resulting in harm or damage to the homeowner. Negligence typically involves two key elements:

- **Duty of Care**. HOAs owe a duty of care to the homeowners in their community. This duty typically arises from the HOA's responsibilities outlined in its governing documents, state laws, and common law principles. The duty often includes maintaining common areas, consistently enforcing rules, and ensuring the safety and security of residents.

- **Breach of Duty**. The HOA breaches its duty of care by failing to act as a reasonably prudent HOA would under similar circumstances, resulting in negligence.

In a negligence case against an HOA, the homeowner seeks compensation for the damages they have incurred due to the HOA's alleged negligence. Such compensation could include reimbursement for relocation costs, property repairs, or other losses resulting from the HOA's failure to fulfill its duty of care. The specific elements and standards of proof required for a successful negligence claim can vary by jurisdiction and depend on the facts of the case.

BREACH OF CONTRACT

Breach of contract alleges that the HOA has violated the terms and obligations outlined in a contractual agreement, typically found in the HOA's governing documents, such as the CC&Rs. This breach of contract may result in harm or damages to the homeowner.

Here are the key elements associated with a breach of contract:

- **Existence of a Valid Contract**. A binding and legally enforceable contract is established between the homeowner and the HOA. This contract typically encompasses the CC&Rs and other governing documents. When purchasing property within the community, homeowners agree to abide by these documents, solidifying their commitment to the HOA's rules and regulations.

- **Breach of Contract**. The HOA breached one or more specific terms or obligations outlined in the contract. This could involve failing to provide certain services, improperly enforcing rules, or violating other contractual provisions.

When a homeowner asserts a breach-of-contract claim against an HOA, they seek monetary damages, specific performance, attorney's fees and costs, and/or injunctive relief. The goal is to make the homeowner whole and ensure the breach doesn't happen again.

BREACH OF FIDUCIARY DUTY

In the world of HOA law, "breach of fiduciary duty" alleges that the HOA board has violated its fiduciary duties owed to the homeowners within the community. Fiduciary duties are a set of legal obligations that require individuals or entities, such as the HOA's board of directors or management company, to act in the best interests of those they serve. In simpler language, board members must manage the community to benefit *all* community members, not just themselves. Fiduciary care represents a heightened standard of care, requiring individuals to act with the utmost loyalty, integrity, and diligence. They must place the interests of those they serve above their own in all decisions and actions.

Below are the common elements that must be met in a breach of fiduciary duty cause of action:

- **Existence of a Fiduciary Relationship**. The homeowner must establish a fiduciary relationship between the HOA's board of directors or management company and the homeowners. In the context of an HOA, the fiduciary relationship is often outlined in the governing documents.

- **Breach of Fiduciary Duty**. The homeowner must demonstrate that the board or management company has breached its fiduciary duties. This breach could involve actions or decisions prioritizing personal gain, financial interests, or other motivations over the best interests of the homeowners.

When a homeowner goes after a board for a breach of fiduciary duty, they want monetary compensation for damages that arose due to the breach, removal of individuals from their positions of authority, and/or injunctive relief to prevent further breaches from happening. Like other causes of action, standards and definitions of fiduciary duties may vary from state to state and among different sets of governing documents.

FRAUD

Fraud claims allege that the HOA board engaged in deceptive practices, leading to financial losses or harm to the homeowner. Fraud is a serious legal allegation involving intentional misrepresentation, concealment, or deceitful actions.

When making the case for fraud, here's what you'll need:

- **Misrepresentation or Concealment**. The homeowner must demonstrate that the HOA or its representatives made false statements, concealed material information, or engaged in other deceptive conduct.

- **Intent to Deceive**. The homeowner must show that the misrepresentation or concealment was designed to deceive or defraud the homeowner. This element requires proof of fraudulent intent, meaning that the HOA or its representatives

knowingly made false statements or took actions
to deceive the homeowner.

- **Reliance.** The homeowner must prove that they took
specific actions or made decisions based on the
fraudulent information provided by the HOA and
were harmed as a result.

Fraud claims can be legally complex, and the burden of
proof is high, as it requires evidence of intent to deceive.
Homeowners considering a fraud lawsuit against their
HOA should consult with an attorney experienced in both
HOA law and fraud litigation to assess the merits of their
claim and navigate the legal process effectively.

IMPACT: IS THE CAUSE WORTH IT?

Impact refers to the question of "harm and damages" at
the heart of all causes of action. These damages may be
physical, financial, emotional, or a combination of these.
When assessing impact, a lawyer usually looks at two factors: economics and quality of life.

Economic impact is easier to parse, so let's start there.
The action or inaction of the HOA is either causing damage to your property or directly impacting your finances.
In the case of a leaky roof at your condominium, the economic impact is fairly easy to quantify:

- How much repair work was needed to the condo unit to fix the water damage?
- How much property had to be thrown out, and what did it cost?
- How long did you have to pay to rent another property while your property was uninhabitable?

Quality of life impact is harder to put into real numbers. These are impacts that change how you live in and on your property. Irritating noises from a nearby venue or continued harassment from the board that cause stress and anxiety fall into this category. These issues could impact your overall quality of life very little or quite a bit. For instance, a venue that's only loud on the weekends might not bother you. However, a growing cascade of dubious fines for an issue you thought was resolved—with the board threatening legal action against you—might impact you quite a bit.

There's no perfect way to measure this type of impact. However, suppose a reasonable person would agree that the situation would chronically disrupt a person's life, leading to negative consequences to their health, livelihood, or time. In that case, it's probably safe to say you've been impacted. To test this, here are some examples of the kinds of questions you can ask:

- Would another neighbor in the community really see the decorative boulders just outside the playground area as a major safety hazard for their kids? Maybe, maybe not.

- Would a neighbor view the large wasp's nest by the pool that's been there for weeks as a hazard to your child's health and an obstacle to the safe use of that amenity? Most certainly.

- Are you experiencing discrimination? Are you a target? An exception? Treated differently? Does your treatment go against a stated rule in the CC&Rs, as specified in the governing documents? Would a neighbor agree that your treatment was unfair? Probably—especially if they've witnessed this poor treatment or experienced something similar.

For any questions you might ask, if the answer is "yes" and redressing the situation is worth it, you've now established a legal cause to fight for.

At this point, the only question is whether enough time has passed. There's a tipping point between when a board can claim they could still take action and when they have not taken action for so long that they are now negligent in their duties. Once they have passed that point, all bets are off, and you are free to declare war. Reasonableness should be your guiding light in this analysis.

FIGHTING FOR A CAUSE

In the end, the common causes of action typically boil down to the broad categories listed in this chapter. Throw in the economic and quality of life damages these infractions cause, and you have a cause you can fight for.

That said, the journey toward justice is anything but one-size-fits-all, particularly when you are at odds with an HOA that appears to operate outside the bounds of reason. The criteria for a valid cause of action can be intricate and influenced by various factors, including the specific area of law relevant to your case and the nature of the grievances you wish to address.

However, by learning not to speak in terms of grievances but in terms of causes of action, you are far more likely to gain the board's attention. "When are you going to fix my roof?" might not be that persuasive, but "I believe you're in breach of your fiduciary obligation to our community, and I will pursue legal action if you don't address the roof that you are obligated to maintain and repair pursuant to the governing documents" will perk them right up. When you can cite your CC&Rs and bylaws, it demonstrates that you know something—maybe more than they do—and legalese often motivates people to address the issue.

And if your professionalism doesn't sway them? Well, you have all the details and documentation you need to hire a good association lawyer and help them hit the ground running with an elevated vocabulary and an enlightened understanding of your rights as a homeowner.

When you're in the thick of your HOA nightmare, you will feel many red-hot emotions. However, don't use that righteous energy to attack; use it as motivation to put the facts together and build your legal case. How is your property problem a failure of the HOA to uphold its required duties? How is your pain a breach of the community's CC&Rs? Why is the HOA responsible for your problem?

Once you've identified the broken rule, code, or bylaw connected to your issue, you go from victim to plaintiff. Now, you're an actor rather than a passive observer. As the old saying goes, knowledge is power. By growing your knowledge, you've given yourself far more leverage in the situation.

But before you go to the time and expense of hiring a lawyer so that you can be made whole, it's important to understand the many potential paths to resolution. In the next two chapters, we'll lay all those different paths out and weigh their pros and cons.

KEY TAKEAWAYS

- The ammunition you will need in court starts with a cause of action and an objective reason for how and why an HOA board crossed the line.

- Common causes of action include negligence, breach of contract, breach of fiduciary duty, and fraud.

- You will also have to prove impact, i.e., that an HOA's bad actions made a direct negative impact on your finances or quality of life.

"The battlefield is a scene of constant chaos. The winner will be the one who controls that chaos, both his own and the enemy's."

—NAPOLEON BONAPARTE (ATTRIBUTED)

Going to War
Informal Battlefields

FRANK PUTS THE HOA ON NOTICE TO FIX THE drainage problem, or he will seek legal counsel. Finally, the HOA responds, inviting him to an informal meeting on July 19. Frank obliges.

At the meeting, Frank is discouraged by the board members' conduct. Two of the members, in particular, keep pushing back. They refuse to accept that the HOA is obligated to repair the greenbelt's drainage system and Frank's damaged home.

Worse, they don't understand Frank's urgency in fixing this issue. "It's just water," one of them says. Conveniently, this board member lives on the opposite side of the community, nowhere near the greenbelt. Without seeing the issue, he doesn't understand the amount of damage that standing water and bad drainage can do.

The meeting adjourns, with the board refusing to take any action. Frank's yard continues to have standing water on July 25 and 30.

At this point, Frank is worried.

Fortunately, despite first appearances, Frank is not powerless, and the humans who appear to control his fate are not all-powerful. In fact, their power is limited—and it can be checked. The question is, what's Frank's best option to fight back?

I'll tell it to you straight: a lawsuit isn't the only way forward. If I were Frank, I would consider one my last resort. Even a so-called "slam-dunk lawsuit" is expensive, distracting, stressful, and time-consuming. My recommendation to most clients is to exhaust all other options first.

So, what are those options? That's what we'll discuss in the next two chapters. In this chapter, we'll explore the many informal "battlefields" on which you might engage your HOA, examining their pros and cons, the processes and procedures involved, and the tactics necessary to win. Each of these forums represents a distinct arena where disputes can be resolved and rights can be asserted.

If, like Frank, you're unwilling to take "no" for an answer, it's time to go to war. So, let's start building your strategy.

INFORMAL DISPUTE RESOLUTION

Informal dispute resolution is often the first battlefield homeowners explore to settle their grievances with the HOA. The spirit behind an informal dispute resolution is to force the board and the homeowner to sit together and civilly work out the problem. It's meant to offer a safe harbor to identify grievances, discuss them, and negotiate promptly without the expense, delays, and hostility of going to court.

Regardless of whether it's legally required, requesting an informal dispute-resolution meeting with your HOA is a sound, diplomatic first move. At best, your issue will be resolved quickly and cheaply. (Remember, a good board is both reasonable and professional and will strive to do the right thing.) At worst, the HOA will refuse to help. Even in that case, you win. You'll look good for being the reasonable adult in the room and have documented another good-faith effort to solve a serious issue.

Of course, if your board is populated by one or more of the Usual Combatants we discussed in Chapter 3, they're unlikely to be swayed by your claims. In that case, no amount of pure intentions and reasonable evidence will be effective in solving the dispute. You cannot reason with a board that's dysfunctional, in denial, or both.

Even in this scenario, requesting an informal dispute-resolution meeting may be worth it, as it allows you to assess which kinds of bad actors might be causing the process to go haywire. For instance, you might see a Fool fumbling around, or a Tyrant speaking over the other directors. Maybe there's a Self-Dealer who claims the problem isn't urgent to distract from the fact that there's no money in the HOA's coffers. Whatever the case, this is useful information for you going forward and an outstanding platform to gain useful insight.

Here's how the informal dispute-resolution process typically works.

INITIATING THE PROCESS

Like Frank, you'll make a written request to meet personally with the board to present your issue and seek a resolution. Most governing documents discuss this option in the dispute section.

Your written notification should include an accounting of the parties involved, the nature of the dispute, and a description of your desired resolution. You can also include the history of the dispute. For instance, "I noticed problem A on several occasions and communicated my concern on dates X, Y, and Z. Each time, I received no response." Feel free to add anything else you think is important for context, but remain objective. Big emotions never do anyone any good in negotiations.

NEGOTIATION

When homeowners attempt to negotiate with their HOA, it signals that they are making a good-faith effort to address and resolve their disputes through direct communication.

Again, I will emphasize the term "good-faith effort." Once you are in the room, it's a good strategy to remain calm. Remember, the board members are your neighbors, and their job is to help the members of their community maintain the integrity and value of their property. Going into a room with both barrels blazing might feel emotionally satisfying, but it may set the wrong tone—especially if the board is already willing to work things out. Also, you do not want to give the HOA any ammunition that can be used against you down the road. For example, yelling and screaming at the board (while likely justified) may come back to haunt you. Best to avoid this scenario at all costs.

Documentation and Communication

Throughout the informal dispute-resolution process, maintain clear and thorough documentation, keeping records of all communication and agreements and any supporting evidence related to the dispute. Effective communication is key, with both parties encouraged to listen actively and express themselves respectfully.

FINDING COMMON GROUND

Informal dispute resolution aims to find common ground and reach a resolution that satisfies both parties. This may involve compromises, adjustments to rules or guidelines, or other creative solutions to address the underlying issues.

FORMALIZATION OF AGREEMENT

If an agreement is reached, it should be formalized in writing. The agreement should outline the terms of the resolution, the responsibilities of each party, and any specific actions or timelines to be followed.

ENFORCEMENT AND FOLLOW-UP

After an agreement is reached, both parties must adhere to the terms. The homeowner should monitor and ensure compliance with the agreement, intervening if necessary. Regular monitoring and vigilance can help prevent future disputes.

RESERVING THE RIGHT TO LEGAL ACTION

While the informal dispute-resolution process is designed to avoid litigation, it does not rule out the possibility of legal action if the dispute cannot be resolved through these informal means. You and the HOA should be aware of your rights and obligations and be careful not to waive any legal rights should future intervention become necessary.

PROS OF INFORMAL DISPUTE RESOLUTION

Attempting to negotiate a resolution with a bad HOA informally can have several potential advantages for homeowners. Here are some of the pros of pursuing informal dispute resolution:

- **Cost-Effectiveness**. Negotiation is typically free other than your time. Homeowners can avoid legal fees, court costs, and other expenses associated with litigation or arbitration.

- **Timeliness**. Informal negotiation often leads to quicker resolutions than lengthy legal processes. Parties can schedule meetings at their convenience, avoiding the backlogs that plague court dockets. Getting resolutions sooner rather than later prevents issues from escalating into more significant conflicts, potentially saving both time and money on bigger legal battles in the long run.

- **Control**. Homeowners actively participate in dispute resolution, proposing and negotiating tailored solutions for a more satisfactory outcome rather than relinquishing control and relying solely on a judge's decision.

- **Less Stress**. Negotiation in a non-adversarial space is generally less stressful and emotionally draining than going through a formal legal process, which can be emotionally taxing for all parties involved.

- **Flexibility**. Negotiations have fewer restrictions than courtrooms, allowing for creative problem-solving that can lead to unique solutions.

- **Ability to Resolve Specific Issues**. Negotiation allows homeowners to address specific issues or concerns without challenging the entire HOA's policies or decisions.

The pros of informal negotiation can help restore, maintain, or enhance community harmony by allowing homeowners to work collaboratively with the HOA and preventing animosity and potential conflicts with neighbors. Through finding common ground and addressing underlying issues, homeowners can contribute to a more peaceful living environment.

CONS OF INFORMAL DISPUTE RESOLUTION

While attempting to negotiate a resolution with a bad HOA informally has its advantages, it also comes with potential disadvantages. These include the following:

- **Dependence on the HOA's Cooperation**. The success of negotiation relies on the HOA's willingness to engage in good faith. If the HOA is not receptive to negotiation, lacks transparency, or withdraws from negotiations early, homeowners' efforts may be in vain.

- **Lack of Expertise**. Homeowners may need more legal knowledge and negotiating skills to advocate for their rights and interests effectively during negotiations. This can put them at a disadvantage when facing a more experienced board.

- **Absence of Precedent**. Informal negotiations do not establish legal precedents that can guide future interactions or disputes within the community. Without legal precedents, similar issues may arise in the future without a clear framework for resolution.

- **No Public Record**. Negotiation offers privacy, but that isn't always a good thing. Keeping a dispute behind closed doors potentially limits transparency and accountability within the community.

- **Lack of Legal Enforcement**. Informal negotiations typically have a different legal enforceability than formal agreements or court orders. If the HOA fails to adhere to negotiated terms, homeowners may have limited recourse to enforce the agreement.

- **Limited Legal Protections**. Homeowners may receive different legal protections in informal negotiation than they would in a formal legal proceeding. The absence of legal oversight can leave them vulnerable to potential unfair treatment or agreements that do not adequately protect their rights.

- **Potential for One-Sided Outcomes**. If the HOA has a strong bargaining position or is abusive during the "negotiations," the outcomes may skew in its favor. Homeowners may feel pressured to accept terms that are not fair or balanced.

- **Temporary Solutions**. Negotiated agreements may provide only temporary relief from disputes, and issues may resurface. Long-term solutions may require more comprehensive changes to HOA policies or governance.

- **Unresolved Disputes**. There is no guarantee that negotiation will lead to a satisfactory resolution. If negotiations break down or the parties cannot reach an agreement, homeowners must seek other options to settle their disputes.

Given these potential drawbacks, you should carefully assess your situation and consider consulting with legal professionals when negotiating with a bad HOA that is uncooperative, resistant to change, or unwilling to acknowledge its mistakes. It takes two to tango, including when solving problems. Both sides must want to reach a mutually satisfactory fix. If the HOA is acting in bad faith, then informal dispute resolution may be more frustrating than fruitful, in which case you can escalate to the next level of war.

ALTERNATIVE DISPUTE RESOLUTION OR MEDIATION

A big thunderstorm rolls in on August 6. The water in Frank's yard keeps building until it reaches the threshold of his back door and flows into his dining room. His house now has severe water damage, and he is furious.

Frank goes back to the board and says, "I now have $100,000 in damage to my home because the board took no action to fix the greenbelt drainage issue." He records the time and date of this conversation and what was discussed.

"We're not responsible for your bill," a Tyrant on the board replies.

How can Frank recover these damages? What battlefield should he go to next?

One option is mediation, an alternative to informal dispute resolution that involves a third party acting as an impartial go-between for the homeowner and the board. No matter who the mediator is, the process is generally the same: the homeowner and board members show up to face off on either side of the proverbial table in order to settle their dispute.

If the mediator aligns with the homeowners' position, they may be able to persuade the HOA to act reasonably and settle. However, it's important to understand that the mediator does not have the authority to compel either party to take any specific action. Typically, the parties are kept separate during the process, and the mediator facilitates communication by moving back and forth between the sides.

In this way, mediation can put the screws to your association without the financial and emotional investment of a full-blown lawsuit. You've put your gun on the table, so to speak, but you're still interested in settling the dispute civilly. If you are unable to do so, the courthouse is your next option.

Typically, you want to leverage mediation in situations where you can't get the board to agree on a solution to your problem. Such is the case with Frank, who is stuck with a $100,000 bill and getting nowhere with the board. He may have a lawsuit on his hands. However, before going to the extreme step of seeking court intervention, he brings in a mediator as a powerful and economical way to resolve the issue.

DEMAND FOR ALTERNATIVE DISPUTE RESOLUTION OR MEDIATION

A "demand for mediation" refers to a formal written request made by one of the parties involved, typically a homeowner, to initiate the mediation process to resolve the dispute. This demand serves as the first step in the mediation process and expresses the party's willingness to engage in mediation to fix their problem.

Now, suppose a homeowner sends a mediation demand to a board in a state like California, where these types of resolutions are baked into state laws. In that case, the mediated dispute-resolution process is mandatory. The board must agree to mediation, or the homeowner is permitted to move forward with a formal lawsuit. Interestingly, in California, if a homeowner requests mediation and the HOA rejects it while the homeowner preserves their right to seek attorney's fees, the HOA may waive its right to recover fees if it ultimately prevails. Generally, this means that if the homeowner prevails after the HOA's rejection of mediation, they can recover attorney's fees.

If your state does not require mediation as a step in the resolution process, you can still come to it by way of mutual consent. In other words, the board agrees to your request for a third-party mediator.

Here's how a demand for mediation typically works within a homeowners association dispute:

- **Initiating Party.** A homeowner who believes they have a dispute with the HOA—such as a violation of their rights, a disagreement over HOA rules or policies, or any other conflict—decides to pursue mediation as a method of resolving the dispute.

- **Drafting the Demand**. The homeowner or their attorney drafts a formal written document often referred to as a "demand for mediation." This document outlines the nature of the dispute, the issues in contention, relevant law, and the desired outcome or resolution. It may also propose potential mediators or suggest a neutral third party to facilitate the process.

- **Delivery to the HOA**. The demand for mediation is typically sent to the HOA's designated representative or board of directors. It may be delivered via certified mail, email, or other means specified in the HOA's governing documents or applicable state laws.

- **Acceptance or Response**. Upon receiving the demand, the HOA has a specified response period, often outlined in governing documents or state laws. The response may involve accepting the demand and agreeing to mediation, proposing an alternative means of resolution, or disputing the need for mediation.

SELECTION OF A MEDIATOR

The mere involvement of a mediator—often a retired judge or some other impartial, credentialed legal professional—

can spur a reticent board to act. But first, you must find a mediator who will ensure a fair and equitable resolution.

Homeowners should consider the following qualifications when choosing a mediator:

- **Neutrality and Impartiality**. The mediator is impartial. They do not have the power to compel action or render a decision like a judge would in an actual courtroom. This neutrality is essential to maintain the credibility of the mediation process.

- **Experience in HOA Disputes**. Look for a mediator with specific experience in mediating HOA disputes. HOA disputes often involve complex issues related to governing documents, community rules, fiduciary obligations, relevant case law, and homeowner rights. An experienced mediator will understand the unique dynamics of HOA conflicts.

- **Training and Certification**. Confirm that the mediator is trained and certified in mediation. Membership in a reputable mediation organization or association, such as the American Bar Association's Section on Dispute Resolution, can indicate professionalism and a commitment to ethical standards.

- **Communication Skills**. Mediation heavily relies on effective communication and negotiation skills. A skilled mediator should facilitate constructive dialogue between the parties, encourage active listening, and help both parties explore potential solutions.

- **Track Record of Success**. Inquire about the mediator's past work and success rate in resolving conflicts. Seek recommendations and reviews to assess their capabilities and suitability for your situation.

- **Conflict-Resolution Style**. Understand the mediator's preferred conflict-resolution style. Some mediators may take a facilitative approach, guiding the parties in reaching their solutions, while others may use evaluative techniques to provide recommendations. Choose a mediator aligned with your preferences and communication style.

- **Fees and Costs**. Clarify the mediator's fees and costs up front. Discuss how fees will be shared between the parties, as this can vary depending on the circumstances. Ensure that the cost of mediation is reasonable and within your budget.

- **Location and Accessibility**. Consider the mediator's location and whether they offer virtual mediation options. Accessibility can be important, especially if parties are in different geographic locations.

- **Conflict-of-Interest Screening**. Confirm that the mediator has conducted a conflict-of-interest screening to ensure they have no personal or financial interests that could compromise their neutrality.

- **Agreement to Mediate**. Before officially selecting a mediator, the homeowner and the HOA should review and sign an "agreement to mediate." This document outlines the terms and conditions of the mediation process, including confidentiality, roles and responsibilities, and the mediator's fees.

- **Compatibility**. Finally, trust your instincts when assessing your compatibility with the mediator. A comfortable and respectful working relationship among all parties is essential for a successful mediation process.

SCHEDULING AND PREPARATION

Once a mediator is selected, a mediation session is scheduled at a mutually convenient time and a neutral location.

Because of its less formal setting, mediation can be conducted in person or virtually, which can help reduce tension and anxiety. Parties may feel more at ease expressing their concerns and exploring solutions from their home office or a rented conference room than in the board's domain.

Before the mediation session, both parties gather relevant documents, evidence, and information pertaining to the dispute. This material may include HOA bylaws, rules, correspondence, photos, artifacts that corroborate the story of the homeowner's nightmare, and any other relevant records.

NEGOTIATION AND AGREEMENT

During the mediation session, the mediator facilitates a structured discussion between the homeowner(s) and the HOA's representatives. Each party can present its perspective on the dispute, including its concerns, grievances, and desired outcomes. At this point, either side may invite a lawyer to organize and present information in a way the mediator respects and understands.

The involvement of a lawyer for the HOA may raise some red flags, but it's not always bad. A good lawyer acts as the adult in the room, the person who says, "Enough! Let's get a resolution." A lawyer managing a volunteer board of directors can ensure that the board remains on topic and doesn't expose the HOA to further liability. They can cut through the posturing, excuses, and ineptitude to look at the facts and quickly find a fix that incurs the least pain for the HOA.

Remember, these lawyers represent the homeowners association, not the board. In fact, they've probably only had minimal interactions with the board. They aren't interested in personal grandstanding or winning at all costs. They just want to get the job done and return the situation to stability. They'll be able to assess the situation quickly, determine whether they have a winning or a losing hand, and adjust their strategy accordingly.

In our experience, this is how most HOA lawyers conduct themselves during an alternative dispute resolution. Every now and then, however, you'll encounter Rambo attorneys, people who drank the Kool-Aid and align with the board no matter what the issue. These are mercenaries for hire, going after whomever the board says to go after for whatever reason, instead of acting in good faith for the well-being of the community.

That's a dangerous situation, but typically, it's also a lot of bluster. If you have a lawyer well versed in HOA law, discussions with a Rambo lawyer are fairly one-sided. Once they realize their bullying and bravado aren't working, they may quickly back down.

Once both sides have presented their cases, the mediator examines the facts and attempts to facilitate a fair resolution. As these conversations progress, the parties will work together to explore potential resolutions and compromise on key issues. The mediator encourages open and respectful communication throughout, helping parties listen to each other and identify common interests and possible solutions. To help with this collaboration, the mediator may use various conflict-resolution techniques, such as reframing issues, brainstorming solutions, and reality-testing proposals.

This step is where the board members lay their cards on the table; are they acting in good faith or bad faith? Any board knows that failing to agree to terms means the next step is a lawsuit. Since most boards don't want to get sued, they typically negotiate in good faith. However, sometimes members are just spoiling for a fight, facts be damned.

After successful negotiations, the mediator or the parties will draft a settlement agreement outlining the terms for resolving the dispute. The agreement may address specific remedies, changes to HOA policies or actions, timelines for compliance, or any other terms relevant to the dispute. Both parties review and, if acceptable, sign the agreement.

To understand what this all might look like in action, let's return to Frank's story. Frank shows up to the mediation meeting with the following demands:

- The HOA will pay him $100,000 in property damages.
- The common greenbelt drainage must be fixed to prevent further damage within thirty days.
- Frank's attorney's fees must be paid in full.

Frank has also spoken with his lawyer about the minimum payment he'll accept before escalating the dispute to a lawsuit and which demands are nonnegotiable. For Frank, the greenbelt's drainage *must* be fixed to prevent further damage that might affect his ability to resell his home.

There are three potential outcomes from this negotiation:

1. The board raises the white flag and agrees to all the demands. Frank enters into a settlement agreement and is made whole.

2. The board rejects all of Frank's demands, telling him to go kick rocks, which forces him to file his lawsuit.

3. The two parties compromise. Maybe their expert thinks the damages amount to less money, so they only offer to cover $70,000. They'll fix the common area because that's their legal responsibility to the community, but they won't pay for Frank's legal fees.

In the case of the third option, Frank can accept this compromise and enter into a settlement, or he can refuse and proceed to court. Going to court will not guarantee a victory, but it will give him another chance at attaining the justice he believes he deserves.

ENFORCEMENT AND FOLLOW-UP

Once the parties have reached an agreement, they are legally bound by its terms. If either party fails to comply, the other may seek court intervention due to a breach of the settlement agreement.

CLOSURE

With the successful resolution of the dispute, the mediation process concludes. Parties involved in mediation often report a sense of closure and satisfaction, as they have actively crafted a solution that respects their rights and interests.

It's important to note that mediation is typically voluntary, and both homeowners and HOAs must be willing to engage in good faith. Mediation offers a potent and efficient platform to resolve conflicts and uphold legal rights. However, this process remains nonbinding until both parties reach an agreement and formalize it through signatures.

If your mediation cannot be resolved, whether because you can't accept the HOA's terms or a Rambo attorney is stonewalling you, then the case escalates to other legal platforms. We'll go over those options next, but know that each platform's exact legal jurisdictions and powers, as well as the municipal and state laws that rule them, differ by state. An HOA lawyer licensed to practice in your state will be able to educate you accordingly.

PROS OF MEDIATION

Mediation offers several advantages. Many of these are the same as informal dispute resolution, such as cost-effectiveness, timeliness, control, flexibility, and community harmony. However, there are other pros specific to mediation:

- **Homeowners preserve litigation rights and attorney's fees**. In some states, engagement in the mediation process preserves your right to move forward with a lawsuit if needed, knowing you can recover your attorney's fees in the process. If the parties don't go to mediation first, you might waive your right to claim those fees as part of your damages.

- **Bad actors lose their power**. Mediation is also the point at which bad actors get shaken out of the tree and lose their power to control the conversation. Now, the discussion is between two (hopefully) reasonable attorneys and an equally reasonable moderator.

Overall, mediation in HOA disputes promotes a collaborative, cost-effective, and efficient approach to conflict resolution, focusing on mutually agreeable solutions and the community's well-being. It can be a highly effective method for homeowners to address their concerns while maintaining a positive living environment within the association.

CONS OF MEDIATION

The disadvantages of mediation can also be similar to those of the informal dispute-resolution process, such as a reliance on HOA cooperation and participation, unequal bargaining power, and no guaranteed resolution. The following cons relate specifically to mediation:

- **Lack of Knowledge**. The biggest hurdle to this type of resolution is awareness. Homeowners just don't know it's an option to pursue.

- **Limited/No Discovery**. Mediation typically involves limited to no formal discovery of evidence compared to litigation. Parties may not have access to all the information they need to make informed decisions during negotiations or "prove" their case against their bad HOA.

- **Potential for Unequal Cost Sharing**. While mediation is generally more cost-effective than litigation, parties must share the cost of the mediator's fees. If there is a significant power imbalance, the party with more resources may have an advantage in covering these costs.

- **Limited Enforcement**. While some mediated agreements can be legally binding, enforcing them can be challenging, as it often requires returning to court to obtain a judgment for enforcement should the other party breach.

- **Unpredictability**. A legal team could have a 100 percent success rate, perfect facts, and confidence from the mediator that it's the best case they've ever seen, and the effort could still fail. The result might be no settlement if the board digs its heels in because, in the end, the mediator cannot legally force anyone to do anything.

- **Delay in Legal Action**. If the mediation process is unsuccessful, pursuing mediation first may delay legal action. This delay could affect a party's ability to meet deadlines or statutes of limitations.

Mediation has drawbacks. Before deciding on this method of resolution, homeowners should carefully consider the specific circumstances of their dispute and weigh the pros and cons of mediation. Additionally, consulting with legal counsel can help homeowners make informed decisions about how to address their concerns within the HOA.

YOUR FIRST LINE OF DEFENSE

Hopefully, you can resolve your issue through one of the paths discussed in this chapter. Overall, they are cheaper and less risky than a full-blown court battle.

To increase your chances of success, be like Frank. As soon as you notice something off in your neighborhood or your HOA, take immediate steps to stop it from becoming a bigger issue. Take a photo of the problem. Jot something down about what you saw or experienced. Record the problem in some way. The more you document what is happening and how you have communicated with the board about whatever issue you've identified, the more ammunition you stockpile in case you need to go to war.

If you've documented everything and tried to resolve your dispute, but the HOA still can't come to a resolution, there are a few other options available to you, which we'll discuss in the next chapter.

KEY TAKEAWAYS

- Informal battlefields like dispute resolution and mediation should be your first plan of attack since these battlefields often get the job done while saving you time, money, and stress.

- An informal dispute resolution is simply an intentional meeting between the homeowner and the HOA to discuss the issue rationally and attempt to reach a resolution.

- An alternative dispute resolution is an agreement to pursue mediation. The board and the homeowner agree to a third-party mediator, who works with the two parties to reach a resolution.

"Courage is what
it takes to stand
up and speak;
courage is also
what it takes to sit
down and listen."

—UNKNOWN

Going to War
Courtroom Battlefields

AVING EXHAUSTED ALL THE ALTERNATIVES, Frank and his lawyer officially file a suit with a state court that is then announced publicly. After a long legal battle, a trial ensues before a group of Frank's peers. All the assembled facts and timelines are presented before the court, and soon, the jury will decide who is legally in the right and award damages as it deems appropriate.

Frank feels optimistic he will get his $100,000 back.

For a homeowner, going to trial is the nuclear option to remedy their HOA problem. It's not a path taken lightly. Any form of litigation is intense and taxing in terms of money, time, and energy. It can be immensely stressful and emotionally fraught; even the best trial lawyer versed in HOA law can't guarantee success.

But sometimes, to secure peace, you need to go to war. After all, the state will not help you unless you force it to. If court is the only way to get traction for your case and enforce your rights, then so be it.

In this chapter, we'll explore the most aggressive, nuanced—and, yes, costly—ways to go to war against your HOA. Again, while there is no guarantee of success, if you arrive at your case well prepared with solid evidence, then the state can compel the HOA to make things right.

SMALL CLAIMS COURT

Before diving into the true nuclear option, we'll take a moment to explore small claims, which, as a court intervention, can still pack a punch.

Small claims court is designed to provide a simplified and accessible means of resolving disputes involving relatively small monetary amounts. Small claims court caps damages at a relatively low number. In California, for instance, the number was $12,500 in 2024. As such, someone like Frank, who is pursuing $100,000 in damages, could not take his case to small claims court. Said differently, if Frank did file his case in small claims and prevail, the small claims court could only award him $12,500.

That said, for smaller claims, many homeowners find this option appealing, especially if they're comfortable arguing their case, since lawyers aren't permitted to practice in small claims courts. (This makes sense. The jurisdictional limit is too low, and we have no business being there.) That said, in your first consultation with a lawyer, they can advise whether the damages you seek qualify for a small claims court and give you a general strategy when making your case.

The following is an overview of how a homeowner can use the small claims court to settle their HOA dispute.

ELIGIBILITY

With the help of a lawyer (if necessary), determine whether your dispute falls within the jurisdiction of the small claims court. Each jurisdiction sets specific limits on the maximum monetary amount that can be claimed in small claims court cases. As long as the dispute's financial value falls within this limit, it may be eligible for resolution in small claims court.

DOCUMENTATION

Gather and organize all relevant documentation, including correspondence with the HOA, contractual agreements, evidence of rule violations, financial records, and other documents supporting your case. A well-documented case is essential to present a compelling argument on any battlefield.

FILING A COMPLAINT

To initiate a small claims court case against the HOA, typically, you will need to file a formal complaint or claim with the court. This complaint should outline the nature of the dispute, the relief sought, and the basis for the claim. There may be a filing fee associated with this process. Typically, forms, local procedures, jurisdictional limits, and so on can be found on your local small claims court website.

SERVICE OF PROCESS

Once the complaint is filed, you must ensure that the HOA is properly served with a notice of the lawsuit, typically through a process server. This notifies the HOA of the pending legal action and its need to file a response.

COURT APPEARANCE

You and the HOA will be required to appear in court for a scheduled trial. During the trial, each party can present its case, provide evidence, and argue its position before a judge (or commissioner). As stated before, you will be doing this without a lawyer, so it's good to rehearse your presentation of the facts.

JUDGMENT

After thoroughly examining the evidence and arguments presented, the judge will issue a judgment on the case.

This judgment may comprise an award of damages or specific remedies.

ENFORCEMENT

If the judgment favors you as the homeowner, you may need to take steps to enforce the court's decision. This may involve pursuing various collection methods. It's wise to consult with a collection lawyer following a favorable monetary judgment.

PROS OF SMALL CLAIMS COURT

As with the other lower-stakes resolution options, a small claims court offers many of the same pros plus a few that are unique to this particular approach:

- **Cost-Effectiveness**. With reduced filing fees and no requirement for legal representation, small claims court is designed to be cost-effective for both parties. This makes it financially accessible for homeowners who may not have substantial resources to engage in a lengthy legal battle.

- **Informal Setting**. Small claims court hearings are less formal than state court hearings. They are typically held in a small courtroom with fewer procedural formalities. This environment can be less intimidating for homeowners, encouraging them to speak freely and present their cases effectively.

- **Simplified Process**. Small claims court procedures are less formal and complex than those of other court systems. The process is designed to be user-friendly, making it easier for homeowners to navigate without an attorney. As mentioned previously, spend some time on your local small claims website, as it will often provide a wealth of valuable information.

- **Speedy Resolution**. Small claims court cases often move more quickly than cases in higher courts. Judges usually encourage parties to reach settlements or mediate their disputes before trial. This means homeowners can resolve their disputes in a relatively short period, allowing them to promptly address their concerns.

Small claims court can be an effective means for homeowners to seek resolution and redress in disputes with their HOA, particularly when the dispute involves relatively small monetary amounts or specific issues within the court's jurisdiction. It provides homeowners with a simple, inexpensive legal process to address their concerns and hold the HOA accountable for alleged violations or breaches of contract.

CONS OF SMALL CLAIMS COURT

And now, for the cons:

- **Monetary Limitations**. Small claims courts have strict monetary limits on the amount that can be claimed in a case. The specific limit varies by jurisdiction, but it is typically relatively low. If the homeowner's claim exceeds this limit, they may be unable to seek full compensation for their losses.

- **Limited Jurisdiction**. Small claims court is designed to handle specific types of cases, often involving monetary disputes or minor contractual matters. Complex legal issues, property disputes, or disputes involving more significant legal principles may be beyond the jurisdiction of small claims courts.

- **No Jury Trials**. Small claims court cases are typically heard and decided by a judge, not a jury. This means that homeowners may not have the opportunity to present their case to a jury of their peers, which could be a disadvantage in certain situations.

- **Simplified Procedures**. While the simplified procedures in small claims court can be an advantage, they can also be a disadvantage in cases requiring complex legal arguments or extensive evidence.

- **Limited Remedies**. In small claims courts, there might be restrictions on the range of remedies or relief available. For example, a small claims judge may have the authority to order the HOA to pay you a monetary sum, such as $5,000, but they might not be able to mandate that the HOA repair the damage to your property.

- **No Legal Representation**. In most small claims courts, formal legal representation is not allowed. This means homeowners must represent themselves, even if the HOA has legal counsel. This can be a disadvantage if the homeowner is not familiar with legal procedures or if the HOA has legal expertise.

- **Time and Effort**. Pursuing a lawsuit in any court can be time-consuming and require significant effort. Homeowners must gather evidence, prepare their cases, and attend court hearings, which can be a burden, especially for those with busy schedules.

- **No Pretrial Discovery**. Small claims court procedures may not include pretrial discovery processes, such as depositions or interrogatories, which are available in higher courts. This can limit a homeowner's ability to gather information and evidence from the opposing party.

- **Limited Privacy**. Small claims court cases are generally open to the public, which means that details of the dispute and the judgment may become part of the public record. This could impact a homeowner's privacy.

- **Emotional Stress**. Engaging in legal disputes, especially while representing oneself in court, can take a significant emotional toll. Homeowners should be prepared for the emotional toll that litigation may take, even at this level.

While small claims court has advantages, it's also important to know its limitations and potential disadvantages. It may not be suitable for all disputes, particularly those involving complex legal issues or substantial monetary claims. Additionally, the outcome is not guaranteed, and you should carefully consider your case's merits before pursuing legal action in small claims court.

ARBITRATION

The mildest form of litigation is arbitration. It is not uncommon for the HOA governing documents to require the parties to pursue private arbitration facilitated by a third-party company rather than filing a lawsuit in public court. The homeowner and the HOA split the cost of an arbitrator to oversee the case and render a binding decision. Both parties must abide by it and generally have very limited appeal rights.

Arbitration can be a smart route under the right circumstances. However, some argue that it favors the HOA rather than the homeowner because the facts of the case are kept secret from the rest of the community and the larger public. While homeowners might prefer privacy in certain delicate situations, there are also advantages to having the facts of the case revealed in front of a jury of peers who, in our experience, are often more sympathetic to the homeowner.

All that being said, if you find yourself locked into the arbitration process, here's how it typically works.

ARBITRATION COMMENCEMENT

Arbitration commences when one party files a written demand for arbitration with an arbitration organization, outlining the nature of the dispute, the parties involved, and the relief sought. This demand is sent to the chosen arbitration provider, which then confirms receipt and provides the responding party with a copy. The responding party has a specified period to reply, potentially including counterclaims. Following this exchange, arbitrators are appointed, often through a selection process in which each party proposes candidates. Once appointed, the arbitrator(s) will schedule a preliminary conference to discuss the timeline and procedural rules, setting the stage for the arbitration hearing where both parties present their cases.

ARBITRATION PROCESS

The arbitration process may involve prehearing procedures, including the exchange of documents and evidence as well as witness depositions. Unlike litigation, it is typically more informal and expedited.

ARBITRATION HEARING

The parties present their cases during a formal arbitration hearing, which may include witness testimony, exhibits, legal arguments, and expert opinions. The arbitrator presides over the hearing and ensures a fair and orderly process.

DECISION AND AWARD

Following the hearing, the arbitrator issues a written decision and award. This decision is legally binding and enforceable. It may include remedies such as injunctive relief, monetary damages (including attorney's fees and costs), or specific performance.

A note of caution: While not always required, home-owners may strongly benefit from legal representation during arbitration to ensure their rights and interests are protected.

PROS OF ARBITRATION

Arbitration has several pros that also apply to the other battlefields described in the last chapter, such as privacy, timeliness, cost-effectiveness, flexibility, community harmony, and simpler, less formal procedures. The following pros are specific to arbitration:

- **Choice of Arbitrator**. Parties in arbitration typically have a say in selecting the arbitrator or panel of arbitrators. This allows homeowners to choose an arbitrator who has expertise in HOA matters and is perceived as neutral and fair.

- **Binding Decisions**. Arbitration awards are legally binding and enforceable in court. If the HOA fails to comply with the arbitrator's decision, homeowners can seek enforcement through the judicial system.

- **Finality**. Arbitration awards are generally final and subject to limited review or appeal. This finality can provide homeowners with closure and a sense of certainty about the resolution of their dispute.

These pros make arbitration an attractive option for homeowners facing disputes with their HOAs, offering a faster, cost-effective, and private means of resolving issues and enforcing their rights.

CONS OF ARBITRATION

Now for the drawbacks. Some we've seen before—like the privacy and confidentiality that could lead to a lack of transparency and the unequal resources the homeowner may have compared with the HOA. The following cons are specific to arbitration:

- **Costs**. Yes, I know this showed up in the pros, but while some argue that arbitration is cheaper and more efficient than state court, I'm not so certain. While it's true that arbitration can move more quickly than a backlogged state court, it can be just as expensive as state court, as the homeowner pays for arbitration fees and legal representation. For some homeowners, these costs may be prohibitive.

- **Multiple Platforms**. There are different platforms for arbitration. Each has its own set of rules, and the proceedings can get complicated, making this battlefield a challenge for homeowners to negotiate on their own behalf, which is why I recommend a lawyer here, just as I would for state court.

- **Limited Legal Protections**. In arbitration, homeowners may have fewer legal protections than in a traditional court proceeding. Arbitration agreements often specify rules and procedures that may not fully align with state or federal laws, potentially limiting homeowners' rights.

- **Limited Discovery**. Arbitration procedures may limit the extent of discovery (the process of gathering evidence) compared to court litigation. Homeowners may have less access to information and evidence supporting their claims.

- **A Biased or Partial Arbitrator**. While arbitrators are intended to be neutral, there can be concerns about their impartiality, especially if they have a history of being selected by the same HOA or have a financial interest in repeat business from HOAs. This perceived lack of independence can raise doubts about fairness.

- **Inconsistent Outcomes**. Arbitration outcomes can vary based on the arbitrator's interpretation of the facts and applicable law, leading to unpredictable results.

- **Binding and Final Decisions**. While some homeowners might like the finality of the arbitrator's decision, others might find they have limited options if they believe the decision is erroneous.

In summary, while arbitration can offer a more efficient and private means of resolving disputes, homeowners should carefully weigh the potential disadvantages. Reviewing arbitration agreements, seeking legal advice, and considering alternative dispute resolution are essential in determining the best approach for addressing conflicts with a bad HOA.

STATE COURT INTERVENTION: THE NUCLEAR OPTION

This is the option most people have in mind when they think about suing. This option represents a significant move when challenging your HOA; it's the "big kahuna" of enforcing your rights as a homeowner, the most aggressive course of action available. At this point, hiring a lawyer for the long haul becomes essential.

Legally, you don't need a lawyer, just like you don't need a dentist to pull out a rotten tooth. You can take on an HOA in a formal courtroom on your own. Just be aware that the HOA will almost certainly have its own attorney who is well versed in HOA law. You will be more effective with a legal professional who can protect you against pitfalls.

The following is an exceptionally oversimplified overview of the key steps involved in a state court case.

COMPLAINT DRAFTING

As Sun Tzu says in *The Art of War*, "Every battle is won before it's ever fought." Nowhere is this truer than in the preparation and evidence gathering that goes into drafting a complaint. The homeowner, often referred to as the plaintiff, works with their attorney or independently to draft this formal legal document. The complaint outlines the homeowner's claims against the HOA, including the facts of the dispute, legal theories, and relief sought.

FILING THE COMPLAINT

The complaint is filed with the appropriate state court, typically in the county where the HOA is located or where the dispute arose. The court will require the plaintiff to pay filing fees, which vary by jurisdiction.

SERVICE OF PROCESS

After filing the complaint, the plaintiff must serve a copy of both the summons and the complaint on the HOA, notifying them of the lawsuit. Typically, a process server or a sheriff's deputy handles this responsibility, following the legal requirements for proper service.

HOA'S RESPONSE

As the defendant, the HOA has a specified time frame to respond to the complaint. The response to a lawsuit typically includes a formal document that outlines the defendant's answers to the allegations, any defenses they intend to raise, and any counterclaims against the plaintiff.

DISCOVERY

During the discovery process, both parties exchange information, documents, and evidence related to the dispute. Discovery methods may include depositions, interrogatories, document requests, and other forms of information gathering.

PRETRIAL MOTIONS

Before a trial, both sides can make requests to the court called motions. These motions can be about legal issues or rulings, such as asking to dismiss the case, seeking a summary judgment, or excluding evidence.

TRIAL

The dispute proceeds to trial if an agreement can't be reached and the parties do not settle. You probably know what a typical trial looks like: both parties present their cases, call witnesses, share evidence, and make advanced legal arguments. In the end, a judge or jury decides on a verdict.

JUDGMENT

After considering the evidence and arguments presented, the court issues a judgment, which is legally binding and enforceable. The judgment may include orders for specific relief, damages, or other remedies.

PROS OF STATE COURT

Okay, now we're down to the brass tacks of a lawsuit. State court has a few overlapping pros with other options for litigation, such as access to legal counsel and binding judgments. The following are specific to state court action:

- **Legal Recourse**. State court provides homeowners with a formal legal avenue to seek resolution for disputes with the HOA. It allows homeowners to assert their legal rights and hold the HOA accountable for alleged wrongdoing.

- **Judicial Oversight**. State court proceedings are presided over by judges experienced in interpreting and applying the law. This impartial oversight ensures that the case is decided based on legal principles and fairness.

- **Access to Legal Remedies**. State courts can issue various remedies, including monetary damages, injunctive relief, and specific performance orders. This means homeowners may be able to obtain compensation or orders to rectify the HOA's actions.

- **Full Adjudication**. State court litigation provides a comprehensive dispute examination process. Parties can present evidence, call witnesses, and make legal arguments, ensuring that all aspects of the case are thoroughly examined.

- **Protection of Rights**. Homeowners can assert their constitutional and statutory rights in state court, particularly if they believe the HOA violated their freedom of speech or due process.

- **Potential for Jury Trial**. Sometimes, homeowners may request a jury trial in state court. A jury trial allows a panel of their peers to decide the case, potentially adding a layer of objectivity.

- **Appeal Options**. If a homeowner disagrees with the trial court's decision, they may be able to appeal to a higher court or seek a review of legal and procedural issues in the case.

- **Transparency**. State court proceedings are typically open to the public, promoting transparency and accountability in the legal system.

- **Deterrent Effect**. Filing a lawsuit in state court can signal to the HOA that the homeowner is serious about seeking a resolution, potentially encouraging the HOA to negotiate a settlement.

- **Clear Legal Framework**. State court litigation follows established legal procedures and principles, providing a structured dispute-resolution framework.

Filing a lawsuit in state court provides a formal and structured legal process to seek resolution for disputes with an HOA. It allows for a thorough examination of the issues, the presentation of evidence, and a legal determination by a judge or jury.

CONS OF STATE COURT

And now, as we all know, there are a few cons involved when going to trial.

- **Costly Legal Expenses**. Litigation in state court can be expensive. Homeowners may need to pay various fees for attorneys, court filings, expert witnesses, and other legal expenses. These costs can quickly accumulate, especially in complex cases. However, if the homeowner wins, these expenses can be reimbursed at the other side's expense.

- **Time-Consuming Process**. Legal proceedings in state court can be lengthy and time-consuming. Cases may take months or even years to resolve, causing stress and uncertainty for homeowners.

- **Burden of Proof**. Homeowners bear the burden of proving their case in court. This requires presenting evidence, witnesses, and legal arguments to persuade the judge or jury, and meeting this burden can be challenging.

- **Limited Control**. Once a lawsuit is initiated, homeowners have limited control over the legal process. Decisions on scheduling, procedural matters, and case management are primarily within the court's jurisdiction.

- **Limited Resources**. Some HOAs may have substantial financial and legal resources, making it difficult for homeowners to compete effectively in court.

- **Public Nature**. State court proceedings are generally public, meaning that case details may become a matter of public record. For homeowners who value their privacy, this can be a nonstarter.

- **Settlement Challenges**. While litigation is ongoing, settlement negotiations may be more challenging, as both parties may be entrenched in their positions and less willing to compromise.

- **Potential for Counterclaims**. The HOA may file counterclaims against the homeowner in response to the lawsuit, leading to additional legal complexities and expenses.

- **Strained Relationships**. Legal disputes can strain relationships within the community. Neighbors may take sides, and ongoing litigation can create an atmosphere of hostility and division.

- **Emotional Toll**. Let's face it: litigation can take a lot out of you. The entire process is adversarial in nature, and all those motions and court appearances add up, costing time and emotional capital that could have been spent with your family.

- **Appeals Process**. While there is an option to appeal an unfavorable judgment, the appellate process can be complex and costly, extending the duration of the case and adding to legal expenses.

- **Uncertain Outcome**. There is no guarantee of a favorable court outcome. A judge or jury ultimately determines the result of a lawsuit, and it may not align with a homeowner's expectations or desired remedies. Even if homeowners prevail in court, there is no guarantee that they can collect awarded damages or enforce court orders if the HOA is financially insolvent.

You can't approach any judge or jury and throw a stack of evidence at them, expecting it to speak for itself and immediately be awarded full damages. That's not how a complex legal proceeding works. Even a slam-dunk case is not a guarantee that you will prevail. That said, we've typically seen that juries are more sympathetic to homeowners than to HOAs. So, if your lawyer thinks your evidence is in order, the law is on your side, and you have a good shot at persuading a judge or jury, it's a healthy risk to take.

RESOLUTION IS WORTH IT

A resolution at the end of a dispute is a wonderful feeling. In our opinion, a good resolution produces two results.

First, the homeowner is made whole on some level. If the battlefield was a state court, the attorney's fees get reimbursed. The HOA pays damages. The association must follow a court-ordered "specific performance" to fix the roof, address the drainage issue, or cease harassment. The board now has to take the issue seriously. What a relief for the homeowner when the nightmare is finally over! The homeowner can finally return to the quality of life they enjoyed before their troubles started. This peace of mind cannot be overstated.

Second, the association doesn't mess with the homeowner anymore—at all. It doesn't send frivolous notices. It acts promptly on maintenance requests, because it's clear this homeowner will enforce their rights. The ecosystem is balanced, with the association working for and with the homeowner rather than against them. Seen another way, it's like the association was the school bully who finally got punched by the little guy, and now the little guy never gets picked on anymore. "I'm going to stay away from that kid," the bully thinks, "because that kid's dangerous."

When little guys stand up to the bully, they're not just standing up for themselves. They're standing up for all the other little guys. This choice can have a profound effect on a community. A judge or jury trial is public. Word gets around. The HOA loses. If it was a case of malfeasance, the homeowners are now galvanized to oust the bad actors on the board and vote for better people in their place.

And now the association lawyer, who may have only been peripherally in touch with the board members and their comings and goings before, is much more motivated to maintain order and provide good advice to the incoming board members. Finally, a lawsuit also works as a reminder to everyone in the community to take membership on the board seriously. After all, the board affects people's property and lives. Therefore, it had better do a good job.

On a small scale, the homeowner goes to war for their self-interest to seek reimbursement and repair for the impact a bad HOA's actions have caused and to be made whole. On a larger scale, the homeowner is the moral victor, doing right for the whole community by revealing and potentially driving out bad actors from the board, preventing future ills from befalling other community members. Despite the toll, these reasons make going to war worthwhile for many homeowners.

And doing so must be worth it, because hiring a lawyer is expensive. Not only will you need the hope of a good resolution, you'll also need to understand how to choose a good champion for your battles.

KEY TAKEAWAYS

- Most HOA disputes end at the level of mediation. Nobody wants to be involved in a lawsuit, least of all a volunteer board. If a dispute does proceed to litigation, the homeowner typically has three paths to choose from: arbitration, small claims court, or state court.

- Arbitration takes mediation a step further and becomes a legally binding proposition. Here, the board and the homeowner select a third-party arbitrator to adjudicate the case and determine a binding resolution that both parties must comply with or face further legal ramifications.

- Small claims court is primarily for low-stakes cases in which the homeowner attempts to recover roughly $12,500 or less. Lawyers cannot represent a homeowner in small claims court, and the court usually awards economic judgments.

- State court or a full-blown lawsuit should be considered a last resort. It's costly and time-consuming, and even if the homeowner has a strong case, the outcome is far from guaranteed.

"In war, there is no substitute for a great commander."

—UNKNOWN

Retaining a Legal Warrior
Lawyer Selection and Maximizing Impact

FRANK HAS TRIED THE DIPLOMATIC APPROACH with his HOA. It didn't work—it barely registered. So, with no other choice, Frank seeks legal representation from a firm skilled at handling homeowner complaints. During the initial consult, Frank lays out everything he's got—a description of the issue, documentation of the damage, a record of every attempt he's made to speak with the board, and a copy of the HOA's CC&Rs. The lawyer's sharp eyes quickly spot several areas where the HOA is vulnerable. It looks like Frank has a case.

Here's the thing about bad actors on the HOA level: they're rarely very strategic. They're not trying to win a war. They're trying to win battles. By rejecting Frank's claims repeatedly, the board members won a series of early battles, but their ignorance and shortsightedness have left them open to legal liability. According to Section 4.5 of the HOA's governing documents, the HOA must maintain and repair common areas to protect homeowners' property. The board failed to maintain and repair a common area near Frank's property, which caused severe damage to his home.

The primary legal issues in this case center on breach of fiduciary duty, negligence, and breach of contract. A fiduciary duty demands a higher standard of care than ordinary responsibilities. The board's failure to act enhances Frank's case, providing strong grounds to pursue legal action.

As a first move, Frank's attorney sends a demand to the board on his behalf: *compensate Frank for the damage your failures have caused and repair the greenbelt to prevent further damage, or we'll take our evidence, and you, to court.* The homeowner now has the legal leverage to compel the board to act.

Even the board's lawyer acknowledges Frank's case is solid. His documentation is meticulous, and the board cannot deny it knew about this problem or that the HOA was responsible for fixing it. There is no pivot out at this point. Claiming the board members didn't see Frank's emails and requests would support the charge of negligence. It would be cheaper and easier to fix the damage than to fight him.

Frank wins. His house is fixed. The greenbelt drainage is repaired. And the board is now wiser for the experience—even if it learned about its legal obligations the hard way.

All because Frank hired a good lawyer.

Hiring a lawyer to pursue your HOA dispute can be an expensive and risky commitment. You want to invest your money wisely to get the attorney who has the best chance of winning and, maybe not so obviously, who understands what you are going through. Hiring a lawyer isn't for everybody, but if you have exhausted all options, committed to going nuclear, and want a crack-shot hired gun to have your back, here's what you need to know to find and retain one.

A GOOD HOA LAWYER UNDERSTANDS THE STAKES

When a homeowner shows up at our office door, this person has already gone through the wringer. Sometimes, they've been dealing with a bad association for several months—sometimes, for a few years. Often, they're in a state of hair-pulling desperation: frustrated, worn down, and unsure where else to turn for an advocate. They are in the fog of war. Many are surprised to find a group of attorneys skilled at litigating HOA disputes on behalf of homeowners. They're stressed but beginning to see a light at the end of the tunnel. There *is* a way forward. There *is* a path to reparation.

This doesn't mean they're thrilled to be in an attorney's office, of course. Many of our clients view us as a necessary evil. I can't fault them. I'd rather they had a good relationship with their HOA and never had to wind up in my office as well. They don't like the fact that what should have been a simple problem with a simple solution has turned into some big, expensive to-do. They don't like that their supposed neighbors and advocates have turned against them, kicking them in the teeth instead of helping them keep their property safe. So, even as there is tension between each side of the war, there's sometimes tension between client and attorney as well.

A good attorney will accept this tension and form a rapport with you in spite of it. First and foremost, for better or worse, the lawyer is your advocate. A skilled lawyer who is brutally honest and lays out the pros and cons of the case with no sugarcoating or empty promises can help you end the nightmare.

An HOA case is not like going to a friendly neighborhood estate planner, who must amicably sort out the heirs and assets. It's more like triage in an ER. Something bad has happened, and life can't go back to normal until the bad thing is made right. Stress is high. Unknowns loom large. Tempers strain to the breaking point. The homeowner's home—typically their largest asset and greatest provider of comfort and safety—has been threatened. And that's no laughing matter.

Hiring an attorney who understands the stakes and the emotions that go with your case is not a must when going to trial, but it helps greatly. Typically, that understanding indicates that they're well versed in HOA law and know the process and tactics that will increase the likelihood of success. An empathetic HOA attorney understands the quality of life at stake and how to leverage it as part of your overall legal strategy. In that way, they don't just win minds but also hearts.

A GOOD HOA LAWYER KNOWS HOW TO FIGHT WITH WORDS

When a desperate homeowner tired of being a victim comes to us, we show them a battle plan that could potentially lead to victory—and that starts with words. Defeatist language like "This association sucks, and my life is in ruins" becomes elevated to "The association is: (1) in violation of the CC&Rs—specifically, provisions X, Y, and Z; (2) engaged in selective enforcement; and (3) continuing to breach fiduciary obligations." This is the language that gets traction in a legal setting. Language is ammo that cannot be dodged or ignored, the difference between a foam bullet and a real one that can penetrate and cause pain for the board with precision.

Using the language of reason is key to gaining that power, to going from victim to victor. It makes those in power—specifically those with the power to enforce action, like judges and arbitrators—take notice. Perhaps most importantly, it informs the board members that you understand their tactics and are capable of using them to your strategic advantage.

Finally, a strong legal lexicon puts the homeowner in a more powerful position to strategically investigate the issues they are having with the HOA. This is why we spent a whole chapter discussing the common causes of action. The more you can speak the language, the more easily your lawyer can follow along with you.

A GOOD HOA LAWYER TELLS IT LIKE IT IS

Elevated language goes both ways. Much of a lawyer's success depends on how reasonable the other side is. Now, there are always ways to escalate—civilly, of course—and put pressure on a board. Sometimes, it only takes a little pressure before the HOA raises the white flag and the parties reach a resolution. Sometimes, we have to fight. Sometimes, that fight becomes a full-blown war.

War breaks out not because you're on weak legal grounds or the facts aren't in your favor, but because an attorney (who has been weaponized by a bad HOA) or an obstinate board refuses to surrender even when the facts aren't in their favor. We've seen plenty of situations where liability was crystal clear, and we expected a settlement to come quickly. Then, the HOA's legal assassin came in and told us to take a hike. In those situations, we don't blink; we sue. Typically, that action defangs the attorney and speeds things along in our favor—often without a trial.

A good lawyer will tell you what that process could look like, both the good and the bad. The default picture is not wine and roses. It's blood and sweat in the trenches that can last for months, even years. Before a single shot is fired, the expectation of going to trial must be named at the outset. If a lawyer you're considering says the process will be bloodless and simple, that's a red flag. We're not taking picnics to the battlefield here.

A good way to vet a lawyer you're considering is to have them predict the case's outcome. If they predict a slam-dunk outcome or start giving you guarantees, you may want to take your search elsewhere. It's dishonest for a lawyer to say, "You'll win because I've won in the past." Even a lawyer with a perfect success rate in HOA cases can lose the next one.

Instead, look for an attorney who can guarantee maximum effort. For instance, we tell our clients that we can ensure our work product will be top-notch. We can guarantee outstanding advocacy that's strategically aggressive. And we can say truthfully that we're tremendously successful in fighting HOA cases. However, we're also careful to point out that just because we've prevailed historically doesn't mean we'll succeed every time. A variety of factors beyond our control could sway the case to the other side.

A GOOD HOA LAWYER ONLY REPRESENTS HOMEOWNERS

A general rule of thumb when looking for an HOA lawyer is to go with someone who only represents homeowners in association cases. Those who also represent associations possess a mindset that isn't focused entirely on getting the homeowner justice. If the lawyer has a large client base of homeowners, chances are they have the experience and empathy to fight for you. They'll know all the firms and the lawyers in those firms who specialize in association law for both sides, which can offer a strategic advantage.

This principle also means avoiding generalists—attorneys who practice in "all areas" of the law. A dabbler won't be aware of all the pitfalls in the laws or the moves the other side might make, and they can end up hurting your case instead of helping it. You don't want to be in the position of paying for your lawyer's education in this area of law. You want them to know the rules at all levels, what to say, who to go after, and how to plead your case.

To maximize the chances of success, the lawyers on the homeowner's side need to be experienced and know this area of law inside and out. A good lawyer in this field understands the exact parameters of their role, which include the following:

- **Providing Legal Authority**. Attorneys are legal authorities who understand the complexities of real estate law, homeowners association regulations, and relevant state laws. They can help homeowners clearly understand their rights and the legal options available to them.

- **Doing a Cost-Benefit Analysis**. Attorneys can help homeowners weigh the costs and benefits of pursuing legal action. They provide transparency about legal fees and potential outcomes, enabling homeowners to make informed decisions.

- **Customizing the Legal Strategy**. Attorneys tailor their approach to each homeowner's situation. They develop a customized legal strategy that aligns with the homeowner's goals and the case's specific circumstances.

- **Assessing the Situation**. Attorneys can objectively evaluate the homeowner's case, determining whether there is a valid legal claim. They can also help homeowners understand their case's strengths and weaknesses, enabling them to make informed decisions about pursuing legal action.

- **Gathering Evidence**. Attorneys can help homeowners gather and organize evidence to support their case. This may include documents, correspondence, witness statements, and other relevant information to strengthen the homeowner's position.

- **Conducting Legal Research**. What legal precedents, relevant case law, or statutes might apply to your situation? A skilled attorney always seeks relevant context to inform their legal strategy and arguments.

- **Protecting Rights**. Attorneys are dedicated to safeguarding homeowners' rights throughout the legal process, ensuring that their rights are upheld, and demanding that they be treated fairly and equitably.

- **Negotiating**. Attorneys can act as zealous advocates between homeowners and the homeowners association, attempting to negotiate favorable resolutions to disputes so as to protect the homeowners' rights and interests.

- **Litigating**. In cases where negotiation fails or the homeowners association is uncooperative, attorneys can initiate legal proceedings on behalf of the homeowner. They can draft and file legal documents, represent the homeowner in court, and ensure all legal procedures are followed.

- **Enforcing Court Orders**. If the court issues orders in favor of the homeowner, attorneys ensure that these orders are enforced, holding the homeowners association accountable for compliance.

You want your advocate to match this level of knowledge and competency. They know the strategies and defenses HOAs and their attorneys might deploy and how judges respond to certain arguments. In all, the process is a bit of a legal tug-of-war, where the expertise of legal professionals, astute attorneys, and judges comes into play.

If your lawyer isn't up to playing with the grown-ups in this space, the association's lawyer will run circles around them. We've seen this happen more than once when we've been brought in on cases that have gone sideways after the original attorney screwed up—not because they were bad necessarily, but because they went outside their lane of expertise.

Once you find a lawyer with substantial experience in prosecuting associations, allow yourself a little sigh of relief. You now have a legal advocate on your side, someone who can elevate the negotiation between parties to a higher level—with none of the ignorance and raw emotion that may have held up talks up to this point.

Often, having this ally in your court is enough to get results. With a different party in the mix, the board's stubbornness crumbles, and they start to play ball. A good lawyer will pursue these collaborative results. After all, they want to reach a settlement and be done with it as much as you do. And, with the exception of the occasional bad lawyer, the HOA's representation will want the same thing. Most early conversations are rational and neutral, with both attorneys working toward an amicable outcome.

A GOOD HOA LAWYER KNOWS WHAT OUTCOMES ARE POSSIBLE

The most important outcome for a homeowner's HOA dispute is a permanent resolution.

However, resolutions do *not* always mean getting everything you want. What you may perceive as a just outcome doesn't always comply with the law. Just because Frank wants $10 million in damages for a $100,000 problem, for instance, that doesn't mean he will get it. A good lawyer will help you tailor your desired outcomes to the maximum you can get.

Such an approach isn't just good for setting expectations; it's also strategic. Reasonable demands show that your side is familiar with applicable law and will help you get results faster. If you find a lawyer who says, "I'll get you that $10 million and then some," turn around and run in the other direction. All demands like this will do is open you up to attack and dilute more legitimate claims.

LAWYER SELECTION

Now that you know what a good HOA lawyer looks like, it's time to find one.

The first thing that happens when a potential client walks through the door of our law firm is a consultation. We ask questions to understand the situation and examine all the evidence the homeowner has gathered. Then, we determine which rights were violated, if any, and what the impact of those violations might be. Finally, we have a broad discussion of the strategy we would likely pursue—and which battlefields that would take us to.

Most qualified HOA lawyers will likely follow a similar process. Remember, during these conversations, you vet the lawyer as much as they vet your case. To be strategic when selecting a lawyer, I recommend the following steps.

IDENTIFY YOUR NEEDS

Clearly define your legal needs and objectives. Understand the specific issues you're facing with the homeowners association. This clarity will help you narrow your search for an attorney with the right expertise.

SEEK RECOMMENDATIONS

Ask friends, family members, colleagues, or neighbors if they have had similar experiences with homeowners associations and if they can recommend an attorney. Personal recommendations can be valuable.

CONSULT BAR ASSOCIATIONS

Your state or local bar association often provides various lawyer referral services that can connect you with attorneys who practice HOA law.

ONLINE RESEARCH

Legal directories, websites, and other online resources can help you research attorneys in your area. Look for lawyers with experience in real estate law, community association law, and homeowners association disputes.

READ REVIEWS AND TESTIMONIALS

Review online testimonials and ratings for attorneys you're considering. While not always definitive, they can provide insights into an attorney's reputation and client satisfaction.

CHECK CREDENTIALS

Verify the attorney's credentials and qualifications. They should be licensed to practice law in your state and a member of any relevant bar associations.

INTERVIEW ATTORNEYS

Schedule paid or complimentary consultations with several attorneys to discuss your case. Plan what you'll ask them ahead of the interview, including inquiries about their experience, approach to handling cases, and fees.

ASK ABOUT EXPERIENCE

Inquire about each attorney's experience with homeowners association disputes.

DISCUSS FEES

Get clarity about the fee structure. Understand how the attorney charges for their services, whether by the hour, on a contingency basis, or through a hybrid arrangement. Request a written fee agreement (which is often required by state law).

ASSESS COMMUNICATION

Pay attention to how well the attorney communicates with you during the consultation. For a successful attorney-client relationship, effective communication is crucial.

CONSIDER COMPATIBILITY

After meeting with a potential attorney, do you feel comfortable speaking with them? Would you feel comfortable *working* with them? There's no right or wrong answer here. Trust your gut. If two candidates appear otherwise equal, choose the attorney with whom you have a better rapport.

CHECK THE DISCIPLINARY RECORD

Research whether the attorney has any disciplinary actions or complaints filed against them. You can usually find this information through your state's bar association.

EVALUATE RESOURCES

Assess whether the attorney is equipped to handle your case. What is their caseload? What kind of support do they offer in terms of resources and staff?

UNDERSTAND THE STRATEGY

Discuss the attorney's strategy for your case and how they plan to achieve your goals. Ensure they are committed to advocating for your best interests.

Choosing the right attorney may take time and effort, but it's crucial for protecting your rights and interests throughout a dispute. Don't hesitate to seek legal representation that aligns with your needs and goals.

FEE STRUCTURES EXPLAINED

When considering an attorney, you must also consider how you'll pay for their services. Here, I explore three common arrangements: hiring a lawyer paid by the hour, hiring a lawyer on a contingency basis, and opting for a hybrid arrangement that combines elements of both.

LAWYER PAID BY THE HOUR

Hiring a lawyer on an hourly basis is a traditional and common arrangement. In this model, you pay your attorney for the time they spend working on your case, and they bill you based on an hourly rate. The rates vary considerably from attorney to attorney, depending on experience, practice area, and location.

A lawyer's retainer functions similarly to a security deposit, ensuring that the attorney is compensated for their services. Clients typically use the retainer to cover their final invoice, and if all services are paid for, they may receive the retainer back in full. However, some law firms deduct fees from the retainer as services are rendered, and they may request that clients replenish the retainer to maintain a sufficient balance for ongoing representation.

Pros

- **Transparency**. Hourly billing provides a clear breakdown of how your attorney's time is spent, offering transparency regarding the costs associated with your case.

- **Control**. You have more control over the legal process and can choose to engage your attorney for specific tasks or phases of your case.

Cons

- **Cost Uncertainty.** Hourly billing can lead to uncertainty about the final cost of legal representation, especially if the case becomes protracted or contentious.

- **Financial Burden.** Depending on the complexity of your case, hourly billing can be financially burdensome, as you'll be responsible for paying your attorney for every hour worked.

LAWYER PAID VIA CONTINGENCY ARRANGEMENT

In a contingency arrangement, your attorney's fees are contingent upon the outcome of your case. In other words, if your attorney wins or settles your case, they typically receive a percentage of the amount recovered. This percentage is agreed upon in advance.

Pros

- **Risk Sharing.** Contingency arrangements align your attorney's interests with yours, as they only get paid if you win. This can motivate your attorney to work diligently on your behalf.

- **No Up-Front Costs.** You can pursue legal action without the financial burden of hourly fees or retainers.

Cons

- **Percentage of Recovery**. The attorney's contingency fee is deducted from the amount you recover, which can significantly reduce the total amount you receive.

- **Limited Case Selection**. Attorneys may be selective about the cases they accept on contingency, focusing on those with strong potential for success.

Be mindful that lawyers generally do not work on a contingency basis when representing homeowners, because the recovery of funds in property-related cases is usually intended for repairs rather than significant financial compensation. Unlike personal injury cases, where large payouts are common, property claims often result in smaller amounts that do not support the risk associated with a contingency arrangement. As a result, attorneys may prefer hourly or flat-fee structures for these types of cases.

MAXIMIZING YOUR DOLLAR

Hiring a lawyer who charges by the hour can be cost-effective when done strategically. To ensure that you're getting the most value from your attorney, consider the following tips.

CLEAR OBJECTIVES

Clearly define your objectives and desired outcomes. Communicate your priorities to your attorney so that they can allocate their time and resources accordingly. The beginning of representation is an excellent time to use your new, sophisticated vocabulary to articulate the problem with clarity, free of unhelpful emotion, and to identify clear goals and objectives.

COMMUNICATION

Maintain open and efficient communication with your attorney and provide whatever information or documents they ask for. Collect random thoughts into one email per day, or even one per week, to avoid unnecessary back-and-forth.

STAY INFORMED

Educate yourself about the legal aspects of your case. While you should rely on your attorney for legal expertise, understanding the basics can help you communicate more effectively and make informed decisions.

ORGANIZATION

Keep your documents and records organized. Provide your attorney with well-organized information and evidence to streamline their work and reduce the time spent collecting or deciphering disorganized information. Any jumbled information or documentation that your lawyer has to piece together will only drive up the cost of their representation.

USE OF TECHNOLOGY

Leverage technology for communication and document sharing. Many attorneys use secure online platforms for case management, which can be more efficient than traditional methods.

LIMIT UNNECESSARY WORK

Avoid requesting unnecessary work or pursuing unproductive avenues. Trust your attorney's judgment and advice. Unwarranted legal actions can lead to additional expenses.

ASK FOR ESTIMATES

Request estimates for specific tasks or phases of your case, which can help you anticipate costs and make informed decisions about how to proceed.

CONSIDER LIMITED-SCOPE REPRESENTATION

For certain legal matters, you may opt for limited-scope representation, where the attorney handles specific aspects of your case while you handle others. This can be a cost-effective solution.

When hiring a lawyer, the bottom line is that the more organized and professional you are, the more you'll get out of the arrangement—and the better positioned you'll be to roll with the punches when surprises eventually come your way. Remember, while it's okay to get angry and vent occasionally, always keep the end goal in mind: winning. Keep the information for your lawyer factual, observable, and concise. Get it to them quickly and succinctly when they ask, as every delay draws out the process. Listen and follow what the lawyer advises in terms of presenting materials and your case. Let your lawyer advocate for you. If you've vetted them before hiring them, they'll know the best plan of attack. All this groundwork will give your case more traction.

RECOVERING ATTORNEY'S FEES

When hiring a lawyer, it's crucial for homeowners to discuss attorney's fees up front to ensure transparency and avoid surprises later on. Before proceeding, conduct an analysis to determine whether pursuing legal action is financially viable. For instance, spending $50,000 on legal fees to recover $50,000 in damages means the lawyer wins while you break even—something to avoid.

A good attorney will assess the legal framework surrounding your case, including statutes, contracts, and any applicable laws that outline the recovery of attorney's fees. They will also evaluate the likelihood of success and potential recovery amounts to determine whether the investment in legal representation makes sense. Understanding these factors can help you make informed decisions and ensure your case aligns with your financial goals.

FOREWARNED IS FOREARMED

It's always good to give the HOA the benefit of the doubt—at least at first. But if the board proves to be unresponsive or hostile, well, you don't have to go to war alone. A lawyer with extensive experience advocating for homeowners will know how to attack the other side and give you a fighting chance to be compensated for the damage done. And now you have a better idea of how to make the most of this expense, giving you the best chance of winning your case and getting compensated for those pricey attorney's fees. You have a strategy to move forward.

In the best-case scenario, you hire a lawyer, they fire off one letter to the board, and the whole case is resolved. That's what happened with my association in the case of my mother-in-law's wedding described in the introduction. That scenario isn't a pipe dream; we've seen many instances where the board caved under the threat of a full-blown lawsuit. Fixing the issue is almost always much less effort than a lawsuit, and as long as the facts are clear and the egos are manageable, the board will take the path of least resistance.

In the worst-case scenario, you hire a lawyer and full-blown litigation ensues, which can take a year or longer to resolve. This outcome may seem egregious, but remember, some clients have been living their HOA nightmare for two or three years *before* they even come to us, with no indication it could ever stop. At least in California and Florida, that yearslong timeline shrinks to months if the process stops at the mediation phase, as is the case with most of our clients. Most associations don't want to get sued, so mediation is where the buck stops with many.

Forewarned is forearmed, and now you know when and how to hire a lawyer to settle your HOA dispute.

KEY TAKEAWAYS

- Attorneys are crucial in helping homeowners enforce their rights against a bad HOA, achieve favorable outcomes, and resolve disputes effectively.

- By seeking legal representation from attorneys experienced in HOA cases, homeowners can confidently level the playing field and assert their rights.

- Not all attorneys are the same. For instance, an attorney well versed in real estate law might not be the right pick for an HOA dispute. Do your due diligence and watch out for red flags.

"Speak softly and carry a big stick; you will go far."

–TEDDY ROOSEVELT

Proposed Cures for Bad HOAs

OVER THE COURSE OF THIS BOOK, WE'VE LOOKED at the issue of HOA disputes from various angles. But there's one question we haven't asked:

Does it have to be this way?

Is this continual cycle of war and peace inevitable? Are homeowners and HOAs destined to do this dance forever? Or is there a way to change the conditions so that HOAs function more effectively and homeowners have more paths to defend their rights?

Here's the short answer to that last question: yes, change is possible. However, even though a significant number of

Americans live in a homeowners association and HOA law is a rapidly growing practice area, we've seen very little policy movement.

As of this writing, homeowners associations have all the legislative power. HOA-related lobbies dominate state legislatures, always pushing for new regulations and laws that favor their side. They are well organized, and the big, frequently ineffective management companies we discussed in Chapter 2 often back their agendas. These lobbies have led to initiatives that could potentially harm homeowners.

For instance, in recent years, one alarming initiative we have seen is designed to allow boards discretion in their decision-making, making them less susceptible to court scrutiny. In California, this initiative is called the "Business Judgment Rule" and states that a court can't interfere with a board's decision as long as the board consults a third party as part of its decision-making process.

Our interpretation of this rule is that it's intended to allow HOAs to work more autonomously and with decreased oversight and potential liability, making them, in effect, unaccountable free agents. Under this rule, it's conceivable that a board could make a horrific decision for its community but be protected from liability as long as it consulted a third party. Would this third party be neutral? Presumably, but that might not be true if a Self-Dealer is on the board.

Meanwhile, homeowners haven't been able to fight back on the legislative level. There is no organized homeowner lobby that advocates for homeowners' rights, and one is unlikely to form any time soon. Part of the reason for this lack of representation is passivity, but the primary reason is ignorance: homeowners are unaware of the imbalance of power and, therefore, are not motivated to learn or do anything about it.

However, despite the power imbalance between homeowners and their associations in most states, homeowners do still have *some* power. After all, the CC&Rs are supposed to provide clear guardrails. Homeowners can still leverage their HOA's bylaws and governing documents through the formal complaint process, and there are still plenty of battlefields to pursue this action. No legislation has changed that fact (yet).

But these battlefields shouldn't be the only option available to homeowners. Other methods of advocacy *are* possible. In the following discussion, we'll explore possible approaches to tilt the system back in your favor.

OPTION 1: IMPOSE GREATER CONSEQUENCES

This book does not necessarily advocate for system changes to improve HOA governance as a whole. However, as professional advocates who have worked in the HOA space for quite a long time, I have a few thoughts that I hope will be useful to anyone interested in changing policy at higher levels.

First, to set the stage, there's a school of thought that says homeowners associations need more regulation and stricter legislation. I don't necessarily agree. For one, many of the challenges I see with HOA litigation are not a result of too little regulation. There's plenty of regulation to wade through in this space, from the state level to an individual community's governing documents.

No, the problems don't come from the existing rules. They come from the people charged with creating, upholding, and enforcing those rules. The issue lies with boards that don't or can't care about those rules—boards that don't take the service they provide seriously, perhaps because it is voluntary and isn't a top priority in many of their members' lives.

Perhaps because of the voluntary nature of a board position, additional rules and regulations would be ill-advised. HOAs have a hard time following current state and community regulations. Any additional legislation will just exacerbate the problem and provide boards with yet another set of guidelines to circumvent or ignore.

Further, adding more regulations may not create the intended effect. Instead of deterring HOAs from skirting their duties, new rules may create a situation in which associations become adept at exploiting legal loopholes instead of adhering to the spirit of the law. This dynamic could lead to a cat-and-mouse game of continuously evolving regulations, which may not effectively address the causes of action in a homeowner's dispute.

For these reasons, I don't see homeowners' current challenges with their HOAs as problems that can be regulated away. That's why, instead of turning up the regulatory dial, I recommend turning up the consequences dial. Rather than focusing on more regulation, ensure that the consequences of misconduct are strong enough to make associations think twice before violating the rules. Make the consequences of foul play greater than the potential gains board members might see by skirting them. This approach could help establish a culture of compliance and accountability within HOA boards, which can be far more impactful in curbing misconduct than simply piling on more rules.

After all, as Teddy Roosevelt famously said, successful foreign policy requires one to "speak softly and carry a big stick." In other words, try diplomacy first, but make it clear that you have the necessary weapons to pound the other side into the ground if they screw you.

Stronger deterrents may be that big stick for homeowners. With stronger punishments, a homeowner who perceived misconduct could hire a lawyer to notify the board and use the threat of punitive damages as leverage in negotiations. Such leverage would be a powerful tool in the homeowner's favor.

So, what would these punitive damages look like? To put some ideas out there to improve HOA treatment of homeowners, here's our short list of ideas for deterring a bad HOA:

- **Punitive Damages**. HOAs found guilty of misconduct may be required to pay substantial punitive damages to the affected homeowners.

- **Community Supervision**. Bad HOAs may be required to submit to community supervision, where an independent third party monitors their activities and ensures compliance with legal obligations.

- **Loss of Management Privileges**. Associations may face penalties such as losing the right to manage community funds, make financial decisions, or enforce rules and regulations until they demonstrate a commitment to compliance.

- **Criminal Charges**. In cases of severe misconduct involving fraud or embezzlement, criminal charges may be pursued against individuals within the association responsible for the wrongdoing.

- **Forfeiture of Assets**. In extreme cases of misconduct, a court may order the forfeiture of the association's assets to compensate affected homeowners for their losses.

- **Publication of Violations**. Associations found guilty of misconduct must publicly disclose their violations and the resulting penalties, serving as a deterrent and providing homeowners with transparency.

OPTION 2: EDUCATION

Increasing punishment to deter future misconduct is one thing; increasing education to prevent future misconduct is another.

Since many problems with a bad HOA originate with an ill-informed bad actor, proper onboarding and training for incoming board members may go a long way toward preventing conflict before it even starts. This process would involve educating board members on their responsibilities and how to carry them out, in addition to making potential consequences for bad decisions more transparent.

Such education represents an opportunity to better utilize the resources of the HOA's corporate attorney. After all, if a Fool can't be bothered to read the HOA's governing documents, they're not going to be aware of regional laws—and their consequences—either.

One of the jobs of an HOA attorney is to inform, instruct, and counsel the board to do the right thing. They already know the laws as part of that job. A quick briefing to an incoming board on the major no-gos and the liability of those bad acts could help set the board up for success. Throwing in an overview of what to do instead—including some basic information on the HOA's management structure, guidelines to interact civilly with the community members, and an introduction to the management company—would go a long way toward filling some of the knowledge gaps.

OPTION 3: CREATE BETTER BOARDS

As discussed, bad actors on boards are the root cause of HOA nightmares. If community members have better choices and are more informed about candidates and their qualifications for a board, then the chances of voting for a bad actor decrease.

So, how can this improvement be accomplished? It's a good question—one that merits further exploration. One way might be to create a transparent review system through which bad actors can quickly be identified and voted out. If a community has the power to elect volunteers to the board, it follows that it should have the power to remove them as well.

THE PATH TO A BETTER HOA

While it is essential to have regulations in place, the true strength of deterrence for a bad HOA lies in making the consequences of bad actions significant enough to stop bad behavior before it starts. This approach acknowledges that associations may currently be violating existing rules, which means adding new ones won't change their behavior. Instead, the proposed remedy for bad HOAs focuses on creating a culture of responsibility, competence, and ethical behavior that benefits the entire community, partly by increasing the threat level homeowners can leverage in a lawsuit.

So, if you, as a homeowner, now feel inclined to be that Reluctant Hero and volunteer for your HOA board, sponsor changes to the governing documents to increase accountability, or advocate for larger policy changes in your city or state, I encourage you to do so to ensure your community's ecosystem isn't a place where bad HOAs can thrive.

KEY TAKEAWAYS

- The true power of deterrence lies in creating an environment where the consequences of wrongful conduct significantly outweigh any perceived benefits.

- This approach is essential because bad homeowners associations violate existing rules and regulations, rendering additional legislation and rules less impactful.

- An alternative approach would be to prioritize and/or standardize education and training for incoming board members. Many HOAs don't do this—or if they do, their training materials have been outdated for decades.

"Inaction breeds doubt and fear. Action breeds confidence and courage. If you want to conquer fear, do not sit home and think about it. Go out and get busy."

—DALE CARNEGIE

Conclusion
Take Your Power Back

Until now, you didn't recognize the power you have.

The biggest misconception among homeowners is that the HOA has all the power. But an HOA is merely a collection of volunteers. It's just people.

The real power is the CC&Rs, the bylaws, and the rules that everyone in the community, including the HOA board of directors, must follow.

The real power is in state laws that regulate and support those CC&Rs.

The real power is in the hands of homeowners who hold the HOA directors' feet to the fire and force them to own up to their responsibilities and be held accountable for their bad behavior.

You've never tapped into this power. Never leveraged it. Never gone on the offensive because you've been too busy playing defense. But it's yours for the taking.

Whether you realize it or not, your CC&Rs are there to *protect* you, not hurt you. When an HOA's board members aren't following those CC&Rs, when they aren't complying with state laws, when they're going bad in some other way, you have the power to use this document to right the wrong done to you and bring consequences and justice down on their heads.

And now, after reading this book, you *know* you have this power. You have the knowledge to take on a bad HOA and win.

You know where HOAs came from, their intended purpose, and how they work.

You know why HOAs go bad in terms of their structure and the bad actors that sabotage their governance.

You know how to spot issues and trace those issues back to a cause of action that gets you traction in a dispute.

You know the main battlefields of HOA disputes and the processes they follow.

You know when to bring in a lawyer and some best practices for selecting and working with one.

And you know some proposed cures for the systemic issue of bad HOAs.

Now that you're armed with this knowledge, the question is: What are you going to do about your situation?

When you understand your rights, you can advocate for those rights in a way that fits your circumstances. Sometimes, you can do so on your own. Other times, you will need legal representation to help you review your governing documents, state laws, or any other regulations your HOA might be accountable for following.

Whatever the case, as you move forward, remember that you are not alone on this journey. Your fellow homeowners are allies; together, you can amplify your voices and effect change within your association. By understanding your rights, the battlefields available to you, and the potential consequences of bad homeowners associations, you become a formidable force for positive change not only for yourself but also for your community.

The strength to effect change lies within you. In the face of adversity, remain vigilant and resolute. Through determination, unity, and the pursuit of justice, you can create a harmonious community where homeowners' rights are respected and your homeowners association thrives as a guardian of your shared well-being.

It's time to correct the wrongs done to you. You don't have to remain passive. You don't have to stay in the nightmare. Sometimes, you have to declare war to find peace. And this is the battle plan to do it right.

Whether in war or peace, I wish you success on your journey.

STAY IN TOUCH

If you're looking for more strategies to add to your battle plan, we've got you covered. Tune into the *Bad HOA* podcast through your favorite provider, where we dive deeper into actionable tactics and real-life stories to help you navigate HOA disputes. You can also find us on social media—Instagram, YouTube, Facebook, and X—by following @lscarlsonlaw, where we share tips, updates, and insights to keep you informed and empowered.

For more about LS Carlson Law and our focus on homeowners' rights, visit lscarlsonlaw.com.

Acknowledgments

Thank you to my wife, Jenny, and our amazing kids, Ella, Elise, Levi, and Lane. You are the spark that makes everything else work. Jenny, your unwavering support, boundless energy, and inspiring strength uplift our entire family every day. We are incredibly fortunate to have you as the heart of our home, continually motivating us to be our best selves.

Thank you to my team at LS Carlson Law. We have been on an incredible journey together over the past several years. Here's to creating an even greater impact for homeowners in the years to come.

Thank you to Michael and Jessica Mogill of Crisp. Your legal growth coaching program has impacted my practice in ways both large and small. More importantly, thank you for pushing me to write this book—and for introducing me to Chas Hoppe of Cape & Cowl Media, who helped me shape my ideas and share them with the world.

Thank you to my parents, Sally and Robert. I wouldn't be here without you.

Thank you to Richard Greif, my wife's grandfather, whose courage and sacrifice during World War II continue to inspire. As an Army Combat Medic on Iwo Jima, he faced unimaginable danger, being both hit by mortar fire and shot while serving his country. For his bravery and selflessness, he was awarded the Purple Heart. His legacy of resilience, sacrifice, and unwavering dedication to others remains a profound part of our family's story, and I am honored to acknowledge his extraordinary contributions here.

Thank you to my esteemed grandfather, Dale W. Carlson. In the crucible of war, First Lieutenant Carlson valiantly held the line so that his men could withdraw. Shot three times and left for dead by the retreating adversary, he crawled through perilous open terrain and eventually back to the safety of friendly lines, where he received life-saving care. First Lieutenant Carlson's heroics eventually earned him a Distinguished Service Cross, the second-highest service award behind the Medal of Honor. Thank you for your service, Grandpa Dale.

Finally, thank you to everyone who picked up this book. There's nothing an informed, empowered homeowner can't do. Here's to your continued happiness.

About the Author

Luke Carlson is the proud owner of LS Carlson Law, PC, a pioneering law firm in the battle against bad HOAs. A distinguished graduate of Chapman University, Luke leads a team of world-class attorneys across California and Florida, specializing in HOA law, real estate, and wealth protection. With a commitment to revolutionizing the relationship between homeowners and their HOAs, Luke Carlson is not just an attorney—he is a passionate advocate for homeowner empowerment.

In addition to this book, Luke also offers guidance through his *Bad HOA* podcast, where he dives deep into the challenges that homeowners face and shares insights on how to combat unfair practices. Beyond the courtroom, he is a dedicated advocate for legislative reform and other efforts to overhaul the systemic failures of poorly managed HOAs.

A resident of Southern California, Luke enjoys life with his wife, Jenny, and their four children. In his spare time, he can be found riding the waves along the stunning coastlines, embodying the adventurous spirit he brings to both his personal life and professional pursuits.

.

Made in the USA
Las Vegas, NV
08 May 2025

21877943R00142